D0063840

ADVANCE PRAISE FOR

Priestblock 25487

"Father Jean Bernard's portrait of survival in a German concentration camp is simple, forceful and vivid—and therefore impossible to put down or forget.

It ranks with the great 20th-century personal testimonies against totalitarian violence. Imprisoned and persecuted as a priest, Bernard clung stubbornly to his faith in Jesus Christ, his own humanity and his ability to forgive. *Priestblock 25487* is a diary of Catholic discipleship under extreme conditions that will deeply move all persons of conscience."

– Most Rev. Charles J. Chaput, Archbishop of Denver

"Deeply moving... The simple honesty of this account of one of the most vivid battles between good and evil in human history is as exhausting as it is inspiring. Evil is only a problem for those who believe in good. The suffering of these priests for the sake of the loving God is one of the modern age's glorious mysteries."

– Father George W. Rutler, author, *A Crisis of Saints*

"This book puts a flesh-and-blood reality on the suffering of thousands of priests, deacons, and bishops who were crammed into Dachau's 'priest block.' The story of Father Jean Bernard, imprisoned for denouncing the Nazis, is as compelling as it is heartbreaking. All students of the Holocaust should read *Priestblock 25487*."

– Ronald J. Rychlak, author, *Hitler, the War, and the Pope*

"Gripping! This crisp story of the 3,000-plus Christian clergy at Dachau in 1941 forces me to turn pages quickly, in horror. During Holy Week some fifty priests have their palms tied together behind them, then bent inwards toward the spine, before being lifted on hooks strung up to the rafters, where they hang for hours in excruciating pain. Humiliation, beatings, and contempt are heaped upon them day after endless day. Large numbers sicken and die. In its understated power, this brief book is unforgettable."

– Michael Novak, author, *Washington's God* (with Jana Novak)

"Father Bernard has left readers with a gripping testimony of the brutal treatment the Catholic clergy received at the hands of the Nazis in Dachau. Despite the grim subject matter, the strong Christian faith held by these men is inspiring, and provides a beneficial example worthy of emulation.

Priestblock 25487 is an illuminating memoir... It authoritatively demonstrates that although the Nazis targeted Jews because they were Jews, they also persecuted Catholics, showing a particular hatred of priests."

– William A. Donohue, President, Catholic League for Religious and Civil Rights

"*Priestblock 25487* is an important work—a gripping firsthand account of the persecution of anti-Nazi Catholic clergy. I highly recommend this excellent book."

– Sr. Margherita Marchione, author, *Yours Is A Precious Witness: Memoirs of Jews and Catholics in Wartime Italy*

Priestblock 25487

A Memoir of Dachau

Priestblock 25487

A Memoir of Dachau

Jean Bernard

Translated by
Deborah Lucas Schneider

ZACCHEUS PRESS
Bethesda

PRIESTBLOCK 25487: A MEMOIR OF DACHAU. Copyright © 2004 Éditions Saint-Paul Luxembourg. Translation copyright © 2007 Zaccheus Press. All rights reserved. No part of this book may be used or reproduced in any manner whatsoever without written permission except in the case of quotations in critical articles or reviews. Printed in USA. For information address Zaccheus Press, 4605 Chase Avenue, Bethesda, Maryland 20814.

ZACCHEUS PRESS and the colophon are trademarks of Zaccheus Press. The Zaccheus Press colophon was designed by Michelle Dick. The text is set in Parango.

Library of Congress Cataloging-in-Publication Data

Bernard, Jean, 1907-1994.
  [Pfarrerblock 25487. English]
  Priestblock 25487 : a memoir of Dachau / Jean Bernard ; translated by Deborah Lucas Schneider.
      p. cm.
  ISBN 978-0-9725981-7-0 (trade pbk. : alk. paper)
  1. Bernard, Jean, 1907-1994. 2. Catholic Church--Clergy--Biography. 3. Concentration camp inmates--Germany--Biography. 4. Dachau (Concentration camp) 5. Catholic Church--Germany--History--1933-1945. I. Title.
  BX4705.B46A3 2007
  940.53'18092--dc22
  [B]

                                                      2007038200

                    10 9 8 7 6 5 4 3 2 1

                 Visit our webpage to learn more:

                    www.zaccheuspress.com

Dedication

In memory of my mother and the priests who died in Dachau, above all my friends

Théophile Becker
Jean Brachmond
Jean-Baptiste Esch
Monsignor Jean Origer
Joseph Stoffels, S.C.J.
Nicolas Wampach, S.C.J.

and to all those persons, known and unknown to me, who worked on behalf of my release.

Contents

Preface

by Seán Cardinal O'Malley, O.F.M., Cap.
Archbishop of Boston

In the darkest times of history the Lord has raised up Saints to be a beacon of Christ's redemptive love. The first half of the twentieth century was marked by two catastrophic world wars that changed the course of history. The Holocaust targeted the elimination of the Jewish race within Europe. Hitler's Third Reich was the catalyst to executing millions of Jews. The reality of evil was tangible by the consequence of war.

Most Catholics would be encouraged to learn that several thousand Roman Catholic priests preached against Hitler's motives and personally protected many Jews during the Second World War. These men modeled their lives on Jesus Christ, the High Priest. Consequently, they became a targeted population by the Third Reich. Over 2,000 Catholic priests became prisoners of one of Hitler's earliest concentration camps, Dachau in Bavaria, Germany. These saintly men of pastoral charity are icons of the suffering servant in their zeal for souls. The priests of Dachau were sentenced to the barracks which became known as the Priestblock.

The testimony you are about to read, *Priestblock 25487*, resurrects the memory of these selfless men. Each page rebuilds the foundation of the barracks with testimony of their priestly outreach to the prisoners in the camp. These priests struggled with the same horrific conditions as did everyone in Dachau. The shadow of the Cross will come across all our lives at some point with the pain of suffering. The priests of Dachau remind all of us that suffering is redemptive in Christ Jesus. Sacred scripture highlights for us that where sin abounds, grace abounds all the more. Truly, the grace of the priesthood was abundant at Dachau.

Priestblock 25487 will inspire everyone who reads it with a renewed gratitude for the priesthood of Jesus Christ. We live in an age where and Hollywood and sport figures are held up as role models. Today, we have before us the lived witness of the priests of Dachau who model virtue and lives of faith.

We give thanks to Almighty God for the heroic witnesses of *Priestblock 25487*.

Introduction
by Robert Royal

This story is both ordinary and extraordinary. It is ordinary because Catholic priests and religious were regularly rounded up and sent to concentration camps in large numbers during the nightmare of Nazism in Europe. It is extraordinary, as all such accounts are, because they give us vivid and unforgettable indications of both the depths of depravity and heights of sanctity to which the human race is capable. Father Jean Bernard offers a straightforward picture of how Good and Evil played out around him in his imprisonment in the Nazi concentration camp at Dachau. He takes great pains to be accurate about the ever shifting conditions as he witnessed them personally. His strict regard for truth, even in such circumstances, is itself an implicit rejection of the violence built on lies that the Third Reich inflicted everywhere it could. If there is any truth missing in this moving story, it is Father Bernard's own quiet heroism and holiness, which he is too humble to include, but which we may intuit in his primary emphasis on the plight of his fellow inmates.

People who have not looked carefully at the position of the Catholic Church under the Third Reich may be particularly surprised by this story. During and right after World War II, it was commonly assumed that Christians as well as Jews suffered a great deal under Hitler. Jews were grateful to Catholics and others for such assistance as they were able to provide, and especially esteemed Pope Pius XII, who quite probably saved more Jews from the Nazis than any other single person. That was why Golda Meir, one of the founders and later Prime Minister of the newly created Jewish state of Israel, thanked the pope and honored him among the righteous gentiles: "When fearful martyrdom came to our people in the decade of Nazi terror, the voice of the pope was raised for the victims." Similarly, Moshe Sharett, the second Prime Minister of Israel, remarked after meeting with Pius: "I told him [the Pope] that my first duty was to thank him, and through him the Catholic Church, on behalf of the Jewish public for all they had done in the various countries to rescue Jews. We are deeply grateful to the Catholic Church." But beginning in the 1960s, following a play entitled *The Deputy* by the Communist-inspired revisionist, Rolf Hochuth, there has been a massive attempt to deny these facts and paint the Church as all but a Nazi accomplice and Pius as "Hitler's pope."

One of the advantages of a memoir like this is its concrete evidence that the anti-Catholic smears are false. Pius was quite aware not only of the threats to Jews but the widespread persecution of his own priests by the Nazis. Careful study of the records in recent years has even given us some concrete numbers that were not available to the pope at the time. In 1932, for instance, just before the Nazis came to power, there were about twenty-one thousand priests in Germany. By the time Nazism was defeated a decade later, more than eight thousand of these men had either been threatened, beaten, imprisoned, or killed by the regime. In other words, well over one-third of Germany's priests came into open conflict with the Third Reich. We can be morally certain that the number who, seeing the treatment of their fellows, opposed Nazism in more subtle or quiet ways was even higher.

Father Bernard was not a German. He came from Luxembourg and joined the 2,670 priests who have been documented to have passed through Dachau, some 600 to their death, from Albania, Belgium, Croatia, Czechoslovakia, Denmark, England, France, Germany, Greece, Holland, Italy, Norway, Poland, Serbia, Slovenia, Spain, Switzerland, Yugoslavia, and other nations. Priests were sent to every camp that Nazis had created, either because they had expressed dislike for Nazism or because Nazism disliked them. (Bogus charges of financial misdealing or sexual impropriety were often trumped up, but many priests, like Father Bernard, never knew what, exactly, they had been arrested for.) For some reason, however, the Gestapo particularly favored Dachau as a destination for priests and Protestant clergy, perhaps as a way of keeping them together and thereby preventing them from "infecting" other prison populations with Christianity.

Because in the end the Nazi hatred of the Church and of what they called "negative" Christianity is a spiritual orientation. Both Hitler and Mussolini shared that spirit, but the Italian convinced the German that a direct attack on the Church had historically always led to failure. The case called for delicacy, tact, indirect and subtle means that would not make anyone a conspicuous Christian martyr, but would eventually result in, as Hitler put it, the chance to "crush the Church like a toad." Anyone who looks over these pages will not encounter Nazi subtlety. Camp administrators preferred the most outrageous brutality. Clever attempts at manipulating public opinion, in Germany and around the world, took place at a much more public level. But what we see here is the brutal and sadistic reality behind the misinformation and propaganda.

We lost a lot of what we knew about this history in the last quarter of the twentieth century. In the 1970s Jewish historians were quite energetic and successful in reminding the world about the *Shoah*, the attempted genocide of Europe's Jews during World War II. For reasons that are not entirely clear, Catholics and other Christians virtually forgot their own heroic witnesses and even had a hard time in keeping before the eyes of world opinion ongoing persecutions and martyrdoms of Christians by the thousands in places like China,

Cuba, Vietnam, and the Soviet Bloc. That was why Pope John Paul II made it a part of the program for the Third Millennium, which was celebrated in 2000 in Rome and around the world, to remember the modern Christian martyrs (Catholic, Orthodox, and Protestant). As he writes in *Tertio Millennio Adveniente*, "their witness must not be forgotten."

His words continue to hold a lesson for us today. This little book works against one temptation that those of us who have never had a similar experience may never have felt, but which we may become complicit in by a failure of truthfulness on the order of the author's. Anyone who suffers a trauma of this magnitude or who has come upon such horrors will be tempted to turn away. But to do so always has repercussions, not only for our understanding of the past, but for our very lives in the present and the future. As Father Bernard writes, "Wanting to forget would also be a weakness on the part of those who suffered. . . . it would be turning a blind eye to similar events taking place today, in full view, in many other parts of the world. . . . Forgetting would be cowardice on the part of the people against whom all these crimes were committed."

The anti-Christian currents in Nazism and Fascism and Communism did not entirely disappear from our world with the fall of the regimes associated with those ideologies in the twentieth century. They are still among us today in disguised cultural forms that demand our constant vigilance.

This republication of *Priestblock 25487* is a valuable reminder of the price of failing to be vigilant both for the Church and for the world, because the persecution of Catholics in the twentieth century is not merely a part of religious history. It is an important but widely neglected part of the secular record of our time as well.

Foreword

to the original edition

I unburdened myself of the pages that follow immediately after my release. They were published serially in
1945 in the weekly supplements of the *Luxemburger Wort*.

The conditions described apply only to the time
from mid-May 1941 to early August 1942. It is important to establish this, because the "climate" in the camp
was subject to such frequent and profound shifts that
different periods are not really comparable.

I have agreed to make what I wrote then available
in the present form, without any alterations, in
memory of my fellow priests who died in Dachau —
for we must *never forget* what happened there and in
many similar places. Forgetting would be cowardice on
the part of the people in whose name all these crimes
were committed. It would be a flight from their own
consciences and from the indictment of the world,
showing an unwillingness to make reparations and to

atone. And by not imputing such cowardice to them, we honor the German people.

Wanting to forget would also be weakness on the part of those who suffered. It would mean that even though they could endure suffering courageously, they now lack the inner strength to reflect on what they endured and to assess what it means for their own lives. That amounts to a wish to forget, in order to make forgiveness easier. And finally, it would be turning a blind eye to similar events taking place today, in full view, in many other parts of the world.

Yet we *must forgive*. We must forgive while remaining conscious of the full horror of what occurred, not only because nothing constructive can be built on a foundation of hatred — neither a new Europe nor a new world — but above all for the sake of Him who commands and urges us to forgive, and before whom we, victims and executioners alike, are all poor debtors in need of mercy.

Priestblock 25487

A Memoir of Dachau

In Prison

"What is your position on the German occupation of Luxembourg?"

I had known the question was coming. Everything up to this point had been just idle chat.

This time they had brought me up from my cell in the Stadtgrund Prison at an unusual hour, and had been strikingly courteous.

"I've got your case all figured out now," says Superintendent Hardegen. "I was just in Paris, where I had a few words with your pals Stoffels and Wampach. The two of them have confessed everything, and now they're trying to pin all the blame on you."

Then he leans over very close and puts his hand on mine in a fatherly way. His tone becomes intimate and confiding:

"I can see you're a decent fellow. I'm talking now as one human being to another. I'd like to save your skin . . . You're covering for your two buddies in Paris. But they're not worth it, they set you up to be the fall guy. Disgusting. It hurts me to see it. Just help me out a little, tell me what they're up to, and then I'll do what I can for you . . ."

What a pathetic creature, I think to myself. What would you know about friendship and loyalty? And suddenly the man's attempt to ingratiate himself makes me feel sick to my stomach. Fatigue is part of it, and I'm starting to lose my composure. I'm too nervous to go on playing cat and mouse.

"Let's get this over with," I say roughly.

An ugly expression crosses his face.

We both know at once that the game is up. We adjust our chairs. I sense that I have turned pale.

And then comes the question I have been expecting for the past two weeks: "What is your position on the German occupation of Luxembourg?"

"I accept the repeated promises of the Führer to respect the sovereignty of our country."

"That's enough," says Hardegen in a cold and triumphant tone. He has won.

+ + +

"Pack your things!"

I feel almost sad to leave my cell in Stadtgrund. It hasn't taken even three weeks for me to make friends with my neighbors to the right and left and — without the need for many words — with the guards, real Luxembourgers.

In the courtyard, Hardegen's own car is waiting. The

superintendent drives me to Trier personally. He is in an expansive mood and talks at me without letup for the entire trip—about the coming victory and ruling the world and how the Church will be destroyed. It is February 1941.

+ + +

"Mr. Origen and Mr. Esch have just left, for Berlin." These were the first words I heard on arriving at the prison in Trier. Instantly I knew I would find friends here.

The door has hardly shut behind me when the "prison telephone" starts working. "Who's the new arrival?" The question is passed from cell to cell, through chinks in the wall and along heating ducts. There is a light tap on my cell wall. My neighbor introduces himself: "Bernard Zénon."

I am very pleased to hear this, for no matter how much his and my ideas and opinions may diverge on some points, I have always associated this name with a person who fought sincerely and fairly for his Communist convictions.

The next day we become acquainted face to face— to say the least, since we meet in the showers.

Then I was shifted to another floor and placed in "strict solitary confinement."

+ + +

"Greetings from Mr. Albert Wehrer!"

The words emerge from an SS uniform pushing its way through the cell door. Simultaneously a package flies through the air and lands on my bed. I open it. It is indeed a substantial greeting from a fellow inmate: a real Luxembourg ham sandwich!

It was not to be the last.

+ + +

After three weeks' probation I receive permission to say Mass in my cell, thanks to the intervention of the prison chaplain.

Only someone who has experienced it himself can know what that means. Now I no longer lack for anything. Breviary, rosary, the Bible, everything is at hand. I may truthfully count the weeks that followed among the happiest of my life. I imagined myself as a monk in a Carthusian monastery . . .

+ + +

My neighbor taps on the wall. "Is it true you are saying Mass? —I'd like to say the responses. Would raise your voice a bit to say the prayers? And please knock three times before the consecration."

As I am performing the sacred rite my cell door opens. Cautiously a guard comes halfway in and looks over at the little altar with an expression that is half sad, half full of longing. "I'm a Catholic," is all he whispers. He stays until he hears footsteps in the corridor.

+ + +

"New arrivals," reports the prison telephone. They are Father Stoffels and Father Wampach, co-heads of the Luxembourg Mission in Paris.

We encounter each other only once, in the corridor. "Was Hardegen in Paris?" I whisper quickly as we pass.

"Yes, and he tried to make us believe you had spilled the beans."

We exchanged proud smiles. Nothing more needed to be said.

+ + +

The cell door opens.

The guard pushes a prisoner inside who is equipped with various tools. "This is where the window won't close, right?"

I look at him in surprise, but he is already hammering away at the window frame. The guard goes out and shuts the door.

"You almost gave me away! You intellectuals! You aren't worth the trouble we take over you. Now listen: The 'new' fellow across from you is a Gestapo spy. He speaks Luxembourg dialect and is supposed to sound you out."

"Thank you," I say, touched.

"Forget it," the man growls. Then he knocks on the door, and the guard lets him out again.

"The window is fixed," he reports.

+ + +

"Visitor!"

It's my mother. She looks pale and tired. She has kind things to say about everyone, my brothers and sisters and friends, but not a word about herself.

The guard pretends not to see all the treats she has

brought me. Then the time is up. She doesn't cry. She holds her head high.

I was not to see her again in this life.

+ + +

May 5, 1941. I am awakened at four in the morning. "Get ready at once! You're being moved."

"Where?" I ask.

No answer is forthcoming. But downstairs, in the office where I am signed out, the guard lets his index finger rest, as if accidentally, on the word DACHAU.

It takes thirteen full days to get from Trier to Dachau — going from prison to prison, in the "special cars" of the Reich railway. Someplace different every night, crowded into a cell with between ten and twenty other men, depending on where we happen to end up.

As a "political" prisoner it is unpleasant to spend the night with so many cell mates, not all of whom fall into the category "pure as the driven snow."

But all the same — this happened in Würzburg.

"Hey, it's Sunday. And you're a priest. You can preach to us, if you feel like it . . ."

The group was made up of Catholics and Protestants. They sat on the floor, leaning against the walls. I sat on the wobbly table and preached about what punishment means and about accepting it as atonement and a way to return to the order of things as God intended it.

I have never had such attentive listeners.

Arrival at Dachau

On May 19, at four in the afternoon, the train arrives at the Dachau station. I am the last to get off.

"Well, the Lord be praised," exclaims a huge SS man, who is on the platform to take charge of the prisoner transport.

"For ever and ever, amen," I reply without a trace of sarcasm.

People stop in their tracks. They start to laugh, pleased to see an SS man get his comeuppance. But as soon as I look into his vicious face, I regret my response. It would come within an inch of costing me my life.

+ + +

Of Dachau itself we see nothing. Directly from the station platform we are loaded into a car with hermetically sealed windows. We sense that we are driving through the streets of the town, and then that we are on an open road. Another ten minutes, and we have reached our destination.

Our exit from the car is hastened with kicks and accompanied by curses. I suspect that they want to let us know from the very first minute that this is the start of a new chapter. So far we had been in police custody, among regular prisoners, but now we have entered the special domain of the SS.

+ + +

After being checked over with extreme thoroughness we march through the massive gate and find ourselves in what is known as the "SS town." Large buildings, designed with a measure of architectural ambition, line the streets and squares. This is the SS administrative center for the entire Reich. Further off are the villas where the SS officers live.

The broad avenue leading to the second gate has well-tended lawns and plants on either side. How much blood and tears go into maintaining the insane degree of cleanliness and tidiness in this part of Dachau is not evident on our first glimpse of the shrubs and flowers, however.

+ + +

In a small building outside the gate of the prison camp itself we are handed over to the camp officials. I am presented to every officer in turn with the sentence, "You won't believe what this padre just did," and receive the obligatory slap in the face from each one.

Then we cross a stone bridge over a deep stream that has been channeled to form a moat around three sides of the camp. On the far side of it there is a high wall with barbed wire strung at the top. From a number of watch towers machine guns protrude in every direction. That takes some getting used to.

A passageway leads under the administration building directly onto the enormous assembly yard.

"Eleven new prisoners!"

The gate closes behind us. We are in a different world.

+ + +

The prisoners are assembled for the evening head count. We have to wait. We withdraw into a corner, and I can take in the whole scene without haste.

The inmates are dressed in blue-and-white-striped jackets and trousers, with a cap of the same material. They are lined up in columns according to height. All the rows, with about 250 men in them, are "straight as an arrow." The camp commandant appears, like a monarch in gala uniform. Then he catches sight of us.

"What's all this? Who in the world is that?" I suppose he has never seen a priest wearing a cassock and Roman hat before in his life. I have to step forward. I take off my hat.

"Hat on! March along the front!"

We make it across. "Prisoners, attention! Caps off, eyes right!"

Then the man in charge reports: "12,436 prisoners present and accounted for!"

The admittance procedures continue. All our clothes and the contents of our pockets are taken from us. Next each new arrival is shaved from head to toe and shoved into a huge shower room. "My" SS man turns up the water so hot that I feel scalded alive, then suddenly makes it ice cold. I summon all my energy and act as if I don't notice.

My companions can't manage it. They scream and try to jump out — just the reaction the guards have been waiting for. They shove them back in and so it continues, in and out, in and out, until the sadistic game gets boring.

Now we get a blue-and-white striped shirt, jacket, and pair of trousers, socks (ah!), and "clogs," which have wooden soles with cloth or leather on top.

Next each prisoner is examined inside and out, with the results noted down, and finally has to take a seat to be photographed. The first of us is just finishing this process when he suddenly leaps up screaming. It turns out that the chair seat has a spring-mounted spike in it as thick as a man's finger — a little private joke on the part of the SS photographer.

+ + +

"Together, march!"

That is far easier said than done. We stumble in the clogs and fall over each another; they don't stay on our feet. But it's amazing what one can learn.

+ + +

They are waiting for us in the newcomers' block, a

special barrack separated from the rest of the camp by a barbed-wire fence. The head prisoner of the block looks us over, ready to start hitting us at the first sign from the SS man who has brought us there.

"There's a priest in this group! Guess which one it is!" Immediately I get a resounding slap in the face. The SS man laughs . . . and so do the other prisoners.

+ + +

"In your bunks!"

Supper had ended a long while before our arrival. The fact that we had not been given any food at midday was "overlooked."

Where could you go in the world and not meet Luxembourgers? Suddenly I found myself surrounded by smiling young faces. It was the soccer team from Niedercorn, in full strength! They had arrived a few days earlier. I hear their names and forget them right away. But as I shake their hands, I get a warm and happy feeling.

They stay only briefly, and a few minutes later the order is given to turn in.

+ + +

The bunk room is separated from the day room where the prisoners eat their meals; both are about 30 feet on a side. Rough wooden frames hold three bunks each, one above the other. At that time every bunk still had a sack filled with straw for a mattress, a wedge for a pillow, a real sheet to go over the straw sack, and a woolen blanket that fit into a washable covering or casing.

"New men over here!" There are not enough bunks to go around, so we have to double up. I am assigned a place in the top tier and scramble up right away.

My bunk mate is a pleasant "status quo" man from the Saar region;[1] I can tell from the sky-blue triangle he has sewn onto his jacket and trousers. He shows me how to position myself so I won't fall out. As I wish him good night, I notice that he is already asleep.

+ + +

I lie awake for a while. The snoring that sets in at once all around me is very calming. I sense that these people have already adapted to the surroundings.

And then I think of the soccer team again. They had all laughed and seemed to see being here from the humorous side. No, wrong! They were seeing it from the athletic side. That's it! Here you have to get used to things and adapt, accept the rough camp life whole-heartedly and, as someone put it, become "an old hand" as quickly as possible. No looking back, no regrets, just dive in headfirst. Do the drill, toughen up!

+ + +

"ATTENTION!"

The sleeping men are jolted awake with a shock of fear. An SS man has entered. No one moves a muscle

---

[1] After World War I the Saar region, which had belonged to Germany, was made a protectorate of the League of Nations and administered by France. In January 1935 a plebiscite was held, and more than 90% of the voters favored returning to Germany. Leaders in the campaign for the "status quo," i.e. remaining under French administration, were arrested by German officials.

for a moment. A light flares up. Heavy footfalls between the bunks. I think I can hear the hearts pounding. Have we folded up our clothes properly? Did one of us fear being cold in the night and leave his trousers or jacket on?

"The man with the egg coddler, come forward!"

I recognize the voice instantly. The witty remark is a reference to my clerical hat.

"Here!" I call out, as loudly as I can.

"Get down!" As soon as my legs are dangling over the edge of the straw mattress, he grabs me and yanks me down violently past the lower bunks.

"Are you the parson with the egg coddler?"

"Yes," I answer, as I try to pull myself together. At once someone jabs me in the ribs and says, "Here you say, 'Sir, yes, sir!'"

"Sir, yes, sir!"

"Priests are filthy swine! —What are you?"

Do the drill, I think. On the outside, like an old camp hand . . . Nobody can take away what's inside you.

"A filthy swine, sir!" I bellow at the top of my lungs.

That impresses him. Maybe he wasn't expecting it.

"Carry on!" —Everyone breathes a sigh of relief. The danger is past.

As I crawl under the blanket again, I tell my bunkmate the story of the-Lord-be-praised incident.

"He's out to get you," he says. "We call him 'B.B.' It stands for 'blond beast.'"

After that, I fell for the first time into the kind of deep sleep that exists only in Dachau.

The First Two Weeks

At four a.m. on the dot the harsh klaxon goes off that prisoners call "the bear." The lights flare up in the bunk room. All the men are on their feet at once, terrified of being the last. We aren't really awake until we're in the washroom, which is actually not too badly fitted out. There are two large round basins with a number of flexible shower heads. Nearby are stone troughs for washing feet. The prisoners push and shove until they find a place to squeeze into. No need for soap.

+ + +

Then it's time to make the beds. What a horrible phrase! It sums up the whole brutal idiocy of camp discipline.

A sack of straw is by nature round. Therefore we must make it perfectly rectangular — like a cigar box. I am struck with amazement even as I try to assist my bunk mate. From hiding places the men pull out boards and pieces of wood cut to exactly the right size for this purpose. One prisoner inserts a stick through a slit in the sack to stir up the straw and push it toward the edges, while his mate presses back with a flat piece of wood to make the edges straight. Carefully they stretch the sheet over the now square sack to make precise ninety-degree angles. Then the cover is folded to a width of 60 centimeters (a measuring stick is available!) and placed on top so that the lower edge is 20 centimeters from the end of the bunk, and the cover lies flat the whole length of the bed, rises at a right angle at the pillow and then lies flat on the pillow again. At the same time the fold in the blanket must run exactly parallel to the blue and white stripes of the casing. Besides the straight edges required on the straw sacks, the most important part is to get the "waterfall" right, meaning the place where the cover must ascend vertically at the pillow like a step in a staircase. Finally, since there are ten three-tiered frames lined up side by side, the height of each made bed must precisely match that of all the others at its level.

O hideous madness of an emptied mind! And worst of all—shall I confess? After a while I began to take pleasure in it.

+ + +

Coffee! Two heavy insulated pails come rattling in. All the men line up, with aluminum mugs in their hands. But not the new prisoners. They don't have any mugs yet, and their names haven't been added to the list for the kitchen.

We don't have any bread, either.

"The bread ration for the day is always handed out in the afternoon," someone explains to me.

When did I actually eat for the last time? —Right, in Würzburg, 24 hours ago . . .

"Everybody out!" —The time allotted for morning coffee is short. The "room crew" has to clean, dust, sweep, and wash up. Everyone else has to go outdoors and stand outside the barrack, either barefoot or in socks.

By now dawn has arrived. It's raining, and I feel an unpleasantly chill wind on my shaved head.

"It's always like this," someone explains. "We're at 1800 feet here, and at this elevation in Bavaria there's usually a stiff breeze."

+ + +

The "bear" klaxon growls again.

"Fall in for the head count!" Between the different barracks the lines form and march in precise order along the main camp street to the assembly yard. The newcomers' barrack has its own private tally. We're not worthy to participate in the general one yet. We don't even know the rules for marching, or how to sing, and don't yet belong to a work detail.

We line up on the barrack street, in the space between our block and the next one. An SS man appears and counts the columns. Then we continue to stand there, without having any idea why. I am already soaked to the skin.

Finally, after a good three-quarters of an hour, we hear the squads marching off to work, and we're allowed back into the day-room.

"Newcomers!" We have to answer questions from the prisoner who keeps the records, the clerk. Then the head prisoner for our barrack takes us aside and to start with gives each of us a hard slap in the face.

"You have to get used to that, boys. Otherwise you're lost. I know what I'm talking about. Half the camp has passed through my hands. A lot of them have me to thank for it that they're still alive."

The man isn't completely unlikable. He seems to mean what he says sincerely. He doesn't look uneducated, and has a face like a bird of prey, with a huge beak of a nose. "A Swiss writer," someone had said. "His name is Hugo Gutmann. He's the best-liked barrack head in the camp. He just hits a lot."

"The main thing is: don't draw attention to yourself! Make your bed properly, sing out and march well. For the rest, your thoughts are your own."

Hugo then explains to us how the camp is run. The prisoners are responsible for the daily routine. The SS are there just as overseers and supervisors, and to administer beatings whenever something goes wrong. At the top of the pyramid is the head prisoner for the whole camp. He has thirty "barrack heads" under him, and each of them supervises four "room heads," since each barrack contains four "rooms."

"After three or four weeks with me you'll be ready

for the camp and will be assigned to a barrack. And you (he means me) will go to the clergy barrack. You don't have to work. Your food is better and you get to take afternoon naps. You can pray all day long and there's a daily ration of wine."

+ + +

"Get out of here!" Hugo yells in my ear. The kick he gives me at the same time tells me in what direction I'm supposed to go. I move like greased lightning and disappear into the latrine. It's just in the nick of time.

"ATTENTION!" I hear the men leaping to their feet and chairs tipping over, then all is silent as the grave. Hugo announces, "Room 1," and the number of men present. Then I hear something about an "egg coddler."

In a split second I have my trousers down and am sitting on one of the five toilets. Then I hear Hugo's raspy voice again, as if shot from a cannon: "Gone to interrogation, sir!"

Now someone else has to stand in and take the punishment intended for me. There was probably a coffee stain on one of the mugs, or a knife in a locker with the blade facing right instead of left.

Then there's another shout of "ATTENTION!" and B.B. leaves the room. Is he going to throw a glance in the latrine on the way out? Instinctively I turn my less recognizable side toward the door, put my head in my hands and my elbows on my knees. "The latrine is the only place where you don't have to leap up and stand at attention," Hugo had said.

Just then the latrine door slams against the wall. I don't look up. B.B. stands there uncertainly for a moment; then he growls something like "bastards" and heads off.

"Don't be stupid," says Hugo when I try to thank him. "From now on whenever it's exercise time, or time to get the laundry, always go along. Make sure you spend as little time in this room as possible."

And so it came about that B.B. eventually lost track of me.

+ + +

"Cappy, where are you?"

"Here!" calls someone in a fresh, strong voice, and immediately a lively little figure pops through the door and looks us up and down with such a cheerful expression that you have to like him at once.

He introduces himself: "Capuchin Father Heinrich Zöhren."

"Don't get sentimental, Cappy! Do you know what I wanted to tell you?"

"Yes."

"So what was it?"

"That you don't want to go to heaven, because there are too many priests there!"

"Right. But if some of them are like you, then I might reconsider. Now, take these new boys outside! Make them march, run, do 'up-and-down exercises' and sing. And don't stand here all day? Get a move on!"

"Let's go," Cappy orders.

The last man out the door gets speeded on his way with a kick from Hugo.

+ + +

"Numbers and triangles for the new prisoners," calls our clerk as he comes into the room. I receive two white cloth strips about six inches long with the number 25487 printed on them in black, and two bright red triangles about four inches on a side.

"Sew them on now!" They have to go on the left side of the jacket and the right side of the trousers.

The other prisoners help us out. One produces a needle. Another shows us how to get thread: He slits open the seam of a jacket with a table knife and pulls a thread out of the fabric.

I am not clumsy with my hands as a rule, but sewing on a fabric triangle so that both the jacket and the patch were smooth, and one point went straight down while the top side ran precisely parallel to the number strip above — that had me sweating from every pore. You could have it exactly right when the trousers or jacket were lying on the table, but the minute you put it on everything was crooked again.

+ + +

The arithmetical calculations I was making as I sewed weren't helping my concentration. 25487! At the present moment Dachau had some 12,000 inmates. If I reckoned that a few thousand had been released, that still meant almost 10,000 prisoners had died in the camp.

"Oh you innocent soul!" comments my neighbor. "They've gone back and started over several times already." —He is working on a green triangle. Green means "professional criminal"; black means work-shy and asocial. We also have a pink-triangle man among us; that means homosexual. He had joined the SS years earlier and performed various tasks; then he resigned and was promptly arrested for homosexuality. Under the regular triangle Jews usually have a second yellow one placed upside down, so that together they form a six-pointed star. The Poles have a P written in ink on their triangle, and the Czechs a T, for "Tscheche."

+ + +

New arrivals! And one is from Luxembourg! I make Marcel Noppeney's acquaintance and immediately recommend him to Gutmann.

+ + +

"Bread ration!"

Four men split one loaf. It's good quality, baked in rectangular pans, and a loaf must weigh about three pounds. At the time that didn't seem like much to me, because it was the only substantial food of the day. I didn't yet know that one can also survive on one-fifth of a loaf.

"The priests get one loaf for three men!"

I can't believe my ears.

"That can't be!" I say to Cappy. "We wouldn't accept that."

"Hush, for God's sake!" Furtively we divide our loaf

into four portions and save some for the new arrivals, who haven't been allotted any bread yet.

"Do you think they're doing us any favors?" he says. "Look, there are over a thousand members of the clergy in the camp right now — nearly one prisoner in ten. Potentially it could have a huge influence, especially with so many Poles here. That's why they put the priests in separate barracks, and it's also why they get 'better' treatment. The idea is to make the other prisoners hate them and keep them morally isolated as well."

Slowly I start to grasp the situation.

✠ ✠ ✠

Room 4 is having a singing lesson.

We have to memorize the camp songs, incredibly stupid stuff. A transport of Poles had just arrived, and it was hard for them to learn songs when they didn't understand a word of the text.

Suddenly a frightened voice called out "B.B.!" He arrived by bicycle, rode right up to the open window and vaulted inside.

"Carry on!" —The song was "Madagascar," and the new prisoners had heard it only a few times.

B.B studies everyone's mouth and notices that the man next to me, a Pole about 60 years old, is only pretending to sing. He doesn't know the song yet, or perhaps he is too frightened to get any sound out at all. So B.B. takes the poker from the stove and starts beating time with it on the old man's shaved head. After a few blows blood is splattering around.

Until then I had kept my head bowed over my notebook of songs, but all at once a terrible rage gripped me. I wanted to leap at the man's throat, but I lacked the courage. Or was it my reason that won out? I threw my head back and stared at the monster in uncomprehending confusion. It was an encounter with an utterly alien demonic world. Suddenly I understood what sadism was.

Right away B.B. has noticed my reaction. He stops what he is doing and bursts into satanic laughter. "Ah, the gentleman feels like rebelling, does he?" And then after a pause: "Well, Well! We've met before!"

Then he grabs me by the waist, picks me up and hurls me as hard as he can against the unfortunate Pole. We both slam against a cupboard that tips over backward. I stay where I land, not moving a muscle. I sensed a hobnailed boot directly over my head.

"Sing, I tell you!"

Hesitantly the song resumes: "Oh it's a long way home, a long, long way . . ."

Then the blond beast disappears, the same way he had arrived.

In the Main Camp

"You'll have to leave our barrack," says Hugo Gutmann when he hears the story. "I'll try to smuggle you into the camp ahead of schedule."

He's already managed it by the next day.

"Prepare to depart for main camp!" The names of five clergymen are read out, including mine, although I've only been in the newcomers' block for two weeks. Cappy is also in the group.

Packing is accomplished in short order: Clogs and cap, song pamphlet and pencil, and the two handkerchiefs we were allowed to keep.

Our head prisoner introduces us to his counterpart in barrack 26: "The whole bunch belongs in the hereafter. But those two" — he indicates Cappy and me — "I want to see again."

A good-bye handshake for Noppeney and the soccer players. We will have few chances to see each other again, and there are so many topics of conversation that we haven't finished yet.

I take advantage of Hugo's good mood: "Look after the Luxembourgers for me."

"Will do. But Noppeney is going to have to stop talking about Spinoza."

Cappy and I receive a parting box on the ears, while the others must be content with a kick.

"Together, march!"

We march up the camp street and swing left at barrack 26. A barbed-wire fence surrounds the three barracks of the clergy block, 26, 28, and 30. The sentry opens the gate, and we march into the barrack street.

It is late afternoon. We see no one at the window and don't hear a sound. Yet they are all inside, since they don't go out on work detail. The whole atmosphere is redolent of an appalling disciplinary regimen.

+ + +

"Company, halt! At ease!"

We are distributed among the various rooms. I am assigned to room 3.

Inside about 60 men are sitting motionless around eight tables. The furnishings are exactly the same as in the newcomers' block. The center of the room is occupied by a great stove covered in green tiles, and the two long sides are almost completely taken up by windows. The other walls have sets of open storage lockers against them, five on each side.

The eight Protestants ministers have their own table. I'm sent to join them, since there is no room anywhere else. They don't seem terribly pleased. All the same I made dear friends among them later.

"Is it always so crowded here?" I ask the man next to me.

"Shut up!" bellows the room's head prisoner. "Do you think you can do whatever you like just because Good Friday is past?"

+ + +

Outside a whistle blows.

In an instant everyone is on his feet, running to the rack where the clogs are kept, grabbing his cap from his locker and rushing out the door. Only when we're outside do I learn that we're going to fetch our food.

A Franciscan priest from Hamburg by the name of Brunke introduces himself. "We're about the same height. Shall we carry a pail together?"

We are already lined up two abreast and fall in behind our mates from the other rooms. And we're off! We march into the camp street, where the clergymen from barracks 28 and 30 join us. An endless line moves in the direction of the kitchen.

+ + +

En route I ask the man next to me, "What did our room head mean with his remark about Good Friday?"

"He meant 'the worst is over.' —On Good Friday last year the SS found some pretext to punish 60 priests with an hour on 'the tree.' That is the mildest camp punishment. They tie a man's hands together behind his back, palms facing out and fingers pointing backward. Then they turn his hands inwards, tie a chain around his wrists and hoist him up by it. His own weight twists his joints and pulls them apart."

"So this year before Good Friday you must have been worried that they were going to repeat the same procedure."

"Yes. They threatened us with it for months. Lent was awful. We hardly dared to breathe, so we wouldn't give them even the slightest excuse. Several of the priests who were hung up last year never recovered and died. If you don't have a strong heart, you don't survive it. Many have a permanently crippled hand."

+ + +

"In the kitchen everything has to go quickly, otherwise you get a beating."

The kitchen is magnificently equipped. Huge cooking kettles are polished to a shine . . .

All at once I'm lying flat on my back. My mates help me up before I attract attention. The wet flagstones are incredibly slippery for our wooden clogs. I notice that the others aren't picking up their feet, but gliding along instead as if they were ice-skating. Everything has to be learned.

The two columns of men split and file down either side of a long row of pails, and as we move forward, we look anxiously at the numbers written in chalk on each pail, which tell what barrack it's meant for. Will we be lucky?

Barrack 10. That's not so bad. Heave! The pail doesn't budge. It is terribly heavy. I feel incapable of getting it even past the kitchen door.

They are beating a man in front of me — also one of the new arrivals. I realize this is a matter of life and death. I see that the others are wrapping their caps around the thin, sharp-edged metal handle and do the same. And ready, set, go!

The few steps outside the kitchen door are treacherous. Once past them we set the pail down for a few seconds and quickly change sides. At that moment someone trips over his clogs and slips down the steps; the hot soup spills all over him.

I look away. "Bad burns," says Brunke.

"It's one of the pails for us!" another man says angrily. He was a priest, too.

+ + +

We alternate our steps to keep the soup from slopping over and burning our hands.

I am more dead than alive by the time we deliver our pail to barrack 10 as required.

"You'll see, with a little practice it gets manageable," says my mate, and he was right. After a short time I became one of the best at carrying food.

"It's the only work we do, though it's not the most pleasant work detail. Morning, noon and night we have to fetch the pails and then after the meal carry the empty ones back to the kitchen."

+ + +

We had red cabbage soup.

"But it was pea soup in the pails we carried," I remark to my neighbor at the midday meal.

"That's true. As priests we get a special diet. But don't worry. Soon we'll have pea soup or noodles when the other barracks get cabbage or carrots."

There was about a quart of soup per man and — at that time still — three or four boiled potatoes. It some-. how seemed like enough to me, so I was astonished when my neighbor took a spoiled potato that I had rejected as inedible and devoured it hungrily.

"It's always that way at first," he explained. "When you get here you draw on the reserves in your body. Then suddenly a hunger arrives that can't ever be sated by cabbage and carrots."

He was right. Soon I too learned what hunger is.

+ + +

You have to work fast if you don't want to fall behind when it's time to rinse out our bowls and utensils.

"For heaven's sake!" someone says to me with a reproachful look as I pull my bowl out of the sink. He shows me that it still counts as "filthy."

At that time the soup still had some kind of artificial fat in it, which congeals on the bowl in the cold water and is impossible to get off. If someone has a scrap of newspaper to call his own, he rubs the inside hard to warm the bowl; that melts the grease and the paper soaks it up. Then he takes a needle and scrapes out anything that may be left between the handle and the rim of the bowl.

"You would have been reportẹd for sure!"

On our locker shelf the bowl must stand with the handle facing forward. And you can't slide it in. Oh no, you have to set it down carefully, because the aluminum might leave a mark on the sanded, light-colored wood.

✦ ✦ ✦

"And the poor guy has handkerchiefs, too! Look, you have to put them on the shelf like this. But it would be better to throw them away right now. They only attract attention, because you can never keep them clean."

I dropped them down the latrine immediately — but secretly, since that counted as sabotage.

It felt as if I were severing my last remaining link to the civilized world.

✦ ✦ ✦

"In your bunks!"

So it's true! I am so surprised that we *have* to take a nap that I am almost the last man through the bunk room door. I slip in just before another man, so that he gets the kick from our head prisoner.

The bed to which I've been assigned is a gap between two straw sacks, but just as I'm about to climb in someone tugs at my sleeve.

"Come," says one of my Polish room mates. We clamber up the corner of one of the bunk frames and stretch out at the very top on the bare boards.

"It's hard," he says, "but it's still better than having

to make the bed a second time afterwards."

We can afford to do that only because our bunks are in a fairly inaccessible corner of the room.

+ + +

Nobody falls asleep, since only rarely is there no disturbance during the hour.

"Wine detail! Let's go!"

A dozen men roll out of their bunks. None of them had undressed. That's against the rules, and therefore dangerous, but being the last one ready is not pleasant either.

In a panic they make their beds . . . Since I have nothing to do myself, I help a very old man who is half blind. Later he introduces himself as a professor from a seminary in Cracow. We throw a last anxious glance at the very hasty job and scurry into the day room.

+ + +

As we take our seats at the tables with our metal cups, as quiet as mice, the "wine detail" has returned and is distributing the bottles.

And then we wait, listening anxiously to the screams coming from the room next door.

An SS man must always be present for the occasion. He will turn up at any hour of the day or night, but then everyone must get into "drinking position" immediately.

"ATTENTION!" We leap to our feet and stand motionless.

"Open the bottles!" There are only two corkscrews

for more than 20 bottles. Since everyone is so nervous, nothing goes smoothly, and the barrack officer throws punches and showers curses on us slackers.

"Pour!" Three men to a bottle. It is quite a decent wine from the lower Moselle . . .

The officer walks around and inspects the cups, to make sure they are evenly filled and that no one gets off easy.

"Drink up, you stinking padres!" The SS man jumps up on a stool and watches us all like a hawk. Not everyone is capable of drinking a quarter-liter of wine in one gulp. As soon as our cups are empty we have to hold them upside down above our heads.

One prisoner chokes out of nervousness and falls behind. In a flash the SS man is on him and slams his fist into the bottom of the cup so violently that the metal rim slices a semi-circle through his lips and cheeks, all the way down to the bone. The man is bleeding so badly he has to go to the infirmary.

✦ ✦ ✦

And then the order comes: "Back to your bunks!" —There are still another ten minutes until it's time to get up. That means climbing back into the artfully made beds, which have to made up again ten minutes later, for the third time that day.

"That's a fine kettle of fish your Pope got us into," remarks the Protestant minister next to me when the torment is over.

"Why's it the Pope's fault?"

"He arranged through diplomatic channels for the clergy to be given special treatment. I only hope it ends soon . . ."

"That's what they say," a Catholic colleague confirmed to me afterwards. "But no one knows anything definite."

+ + +

Yet another surprise is in store that evening.

Everyone is already in bed, but the klaxon has not yet sounded. The head prisoner is sleeping in the day room and won't bother us. From somewhere over in a corner one quiet voice begins, first in Polish, then in German. It is the daily summary of the political and military situation. The "reporter" reads from various newspapers and adds some daring commentary. Then we fold our hands.

Benedictio Dei omnipotentis . . . The bishop of Leslau,[1] Monsignor Cozal, gives the blessing. The Protestants make the sign of the cross, too. And we have the feeling that the bishop's blessing gives meaning to our suffering, lifts it above the purely human and joins our small, personal suffering to the sea of injury and persecution that the church of Christ endures and must endure. His blessing lets us share in the graces and comforts and sources of strength that fed the first martyrs.

O miracle of the communion of saints, which becomes our experience here!

[1] After annexing part of Poland in World War II, the Germans gave the name "Leslau" to the district of Włocławek. –Translator's note.

Even our sleep is illuminated by the great certainty: *Et non prevalebunt* . . . And the gates of Hell shall not prevail against it.

+ + +

The clergy get up a quarter of an hour earlier than the other prisoners in the camp. At quarter to four on the dot we are on our feet, shake the straw off, put on our trousers and jackets and set off to get the coffee. We wash afterwards, that is, if there is enough time.

After morning coffee we have to make our beds (and the standard is even crazier here than what I had learned in the newcomers' block), put our lockers in order and then we head outside so the barrack detail can clean the room. Shivering in the cold morning air, we anxiously peer in the window as our room head inspects the lockers and beds. And woe if he calls out a name, pulls a bed apart or tosses the entire contents of a locker into the street! Every morning there are a few bloody heads, meals docked, or even a report to the camp authorities. We can relax only after our lockers and beds have been deemed acceptable.

+ + +

"Almost all the 'head prisoners' are communists," a veteran camp inmate informs me. "That's because they were the first group the Nazis arrested en masse. Some of them have been in the camp for more than five years, and they can hardly be considered normal human beings any more. For that very reason, and because they've completely internalized the camp discipline, the SS leadership thinks they are the right instruments to carry out their policy.

"The 'head prisoners' get more food; they're allowed to use the camp shop more often, don't have to join work details, and are real little kings in the camp. So they do everything they can to keep their jobs and outdo one another in abusing their fellow prisoners. On the other hand if a room or a barrack attracts attention for sloppy marching or singing, for instance, then the head prisoner is the first to be hanged or flogged — 25 lashes on his bare back with the double bull-whip.

"For the clergy barracks they naturally chose prize specimens. The head prisoner for barrack 26 is a monster. Luckily our room head is more lazy than nasty. His name is Emil and he claims to have been an actor."

The clergy are of course — fortunately — not eligible for such posts.

+ + +

"Fall in!"

We march in rows of ten to the morning head count.

The barrack head prisoner calls out the song: "Hazelnut!" And look out if we don't all start singing right away in the same key! Then we'll have to run and do "up-and-down" exercises for an hour, or perhaps we won't get our midday meal until evening.

+ + +

For the head count the three clergy barracks are the last to march in and occupy their usual positions.

I observe that our barrack 26 is the smallest by far. That's because only two of its four rooms are occupied: Room 1 is the chapel, and room 4 is used as a store-room.

I hastily count the number of rows from the clergy block and estimate that the total number is between 750 and 800 men.

+ + +

Then follows the endless scenario of the tally: First of all the rows, with 300 men in each, have to be straight enough that you could shoot a bullet between them. Then we stand there, for half or three-quarters of an hour — for what purpose, nobody knows — in cold weather, in the heat, in rain and snow. Then we're counted by the SS. Then the drill: "Prisoners, attention! Caps off, eyes right, eyes straight ahead, caps on, at ease!" And at long last, dismissal: "About face!" Three times a day.

First Mass in the Camp

Then came the great occasion, the day I had been eagerly awaiting: my first Mass in the concentration camp!

Immediately on returning from the head count we — meaning all the inmates of the three clergy barracks — proceed to room 1 of barrack 26. Here the wall that otherwise divides the day room from the bunk room has been removed, creating a room measuring roughly 30 by 60 feet, with windows on the long sides. Against the wall at the end of the barrack is an altar, made of two tables pushed together and covered with a bed sheet. Behind the altar a cross is painted on the wall. There are real candles on blocks of wood, and a crucifix.

These arrangements are completed before our eyes as the room quickly fills. Near the door is a small plate with tiny pieces of the Host, a fraction of an inch in size, and each man takes one as he enters. We keep squeezing together until finally we are standing packed like street-car passengers on a rainy day.

Mass is always celebrated by the same priest, a former chaplain in the Polish army, the only one who has been given permission. The essential vestments, hosts and wine are gifts from the parish priests in the town of Dachau. The sacred rite commences. It proceeds in haste, and the gathering is uneasy and nervous. Everyone knows that Mass is tolerated rather than really allowed, and each time it could be disrupted.

The head prisoner of the barrack stands at the rear, his cap on his head; we sense he is just looking for a pretext to create a disturbance.

The celebrant speaks the prayers of the Mass in a loud voice, and the others whisper them in accompaniment. At the offering we raise our hands with the tiny bit of Host. Before the transubstantiation someone plucks at my sleeve. "*Prosze,*" he says in Polish, "please." Then he puts his particle of Host in my hand, next to my own. I gather that he is not a priest, perhaps only a seminarian or monk, for the celebrant's intention is to consecrate all the pieces of Host that are being held by priests.

"*Hoc est corpus meum.*" I look at the two bits of Host in my hand, and as the One for Whom we are suffering all this comes into our midst, as in their hearts hundreds of priests join their offering with that of the Savior, tears roll down my cheeks. It becomes a single offering that certainly creates new ties between heaven and earth.

For Holy Communion the priests gather the pieces

together; the communicants are the non-priests who entrusted a small bit of the Host to them.

It is a sea of comfort that pours out over the gathering. Comfort and hope and strength for new suffering joyfully accepted.

+ + +

"Lice inspection!" shouts the barrack head as we give thanks. Hastily things are cleared away, and everyone surges toward the exit.

In our room the head prisoner is already sitting on a stool, posed self-importantly with his list of names and a pencil. Everyone must strip naked and file one after another past His Majesty. The inspection requires a particularly thorough search of certain parts of the body, to make sure that no trace of lice or scabies has been overlooked.

Occasionally our room head takes special pleasure in inviting a colleague from another barrack to attend the performance. The guest has nothing else to do, since his prisoners are out on work detail. The jokes they make are not fit to be repeated.

"How often are these scenes put on?" I ask a fellow prisoner.

"In the other barracks now and then on a Sunday at most. Here, there's an inspection nearly every day. The clergy seem to be particularly susceptible to such infestations."

But what harm does it do? We have heaven in our hearts, and the Lord resides next door (in a drawer), in our midst.

Recollections From the
First Few Months

Now I ask the reader's indulgence if I relate only a few events from the next four months, occurrences that seem typical of life in the concentration camp and the atmosphere there.

There is a saying that nations without a history are happy nations. It is in this sense the next few more or less uneventful months can be described "happy." They were "paradise" compared with what followed. If you were healthy and robust and hadn't become too soft, if you had retained some of the ability of the young to adapt quickly, if you had a healthy sense of optimism — and a little good luck — you could make it through.

+ + +

Letter-writing time.

In principle that was every other Sunday. The Luxembourgers and the Dutch had to write their letters on plain white paper, while the Germans and Poles used official camp stationery. I never learned the reason for this.

First I wrote a draft and showed it to a seasoned inmate. "My God!" he exclaimed and crossed out half of it.

I made another attempt, and once again the most interesting bits failed to pass the unofficial censorship test.

And when I finally found the acceptable style of writing, my letter looked more or less like all letters from then on. It consisted of a few sentences that revealed not much more than the fact that I was still alive:

Dear Mother, I received your letter. I am well. I'm healthy and in good spirits. I don't need anything. Send me a few stamps and some money for my account here, in case there might be something to buy in the camp shop . . .

+ + +

We are just washing the dishes when we hear a racket going on outside. Hugo Gutmann and the head prisoner of our room are beating up a wretched creature while an SS man stands nearby laughing.

"The son of a bitch had the nerve to give the Hitler salute!"

"Don't you know prisoners aren't allowed to?" I recognize the unlucky devil. He's an elderly Protestant pastor I met in the newcomers' block. His name is Berndt, and he seems like a very soft fellow. One of his sons, a volunteer, has already been killed in the war, and another son is a high-ranking SS officer. The pastor simply can't come to terms with his arrest, and keeps hoping he'll be able to save himself with political gestures.

The man will not survive. Even I know that much about the camp by now.

+ + +

"Fall in for the showers!"

In a flash we are outside with our towels and soap. The showers are next to the kitchen. We march in lock-step, singing, until we reach the entrance. Then we wait until it's our turn to go in.

As soon as it is we storm inside, for the goal is to seize possession of a clothes hook and make maximum use of the few minutes at our disposal. The experienced prisoners have already stripped naked by the time they reach the hook they had their eye on.

Only the first few times does one feel anything like shame. After that the pleasant feeling of being clean outweighs everything else. The shower room was designed for "only" 300 men, so several prisoners have to share a shower head.

The water is wonderfully warm. But after only a few minutes the temperature switches to icy cold. Some men try to jump out of the way, but if the head prisoner of our barrack happens to be in the mood for it that day, he sprays them with a separate hose.

As I am getting dressed, I notice that there are massive iron hooks screwed into the rafters above us.

"That's where they hang the men who are sentenced to one or two hours of the 'tree' as punishment. It's where the sixty priests were hoisted up on Good Friday . . ."

+ + +

On the march back we botch the beginning of the song we are ordered to sing. At the same time the head prisoner for the barrack thinks he sees the curtains moving at the camp commandant's window.

His commands become uncertain, and nothing goes right. Promptly the camp runner arrives with an order: Do "up-and-down" exercises until head-count time!

It is terribly hot, and as we run we stir up unbearable clouds of dust in the parched assembly yard.

Run, throw yourself flat on your stomach, stand up! Soon we are covered in a layer of dirt and sweat like a suit of armor. Until the next shower day.

Three men faint and end up in the infirmary.

+ + +

Two days in a row we did not get our wine for some reason or other. On the third day we therefore had to gulp down a triple ration . . . Meaning three-quarters of a liter, a bottle each, almost without a break. It was torment of a unique kind, and hardly anyone was sober at the end of it.

Then the SS and our room head enjoyed a good laugh together about the drunken pack of priests.

+ + +

Room 4 is supposed to be occupied soon. Up to now it has served as a storage room for the camp band's instruments.

I volunteer for the work detail to get it ready; there is carpentry and metal work to do. It means I can escape the torment of the room head for a few days, and time passes more quickly.

Furthermore the head prisoner for the new room has already been chosen. He is quite a decent fellow, and I entertain the hope that he will let me transfer.

But the situation also has a negative side: When the musical instruments are moved I will lose my only contact with the rest of the camp. Kauthen, the saxophone player, comes from Luxembourg, and he is allowed to enter the clergy block because he often comes to check on the instruments — meaning whenever there is any news regarding the Luxembourg contingent that he wants to pass on to me.

+ + +

Breviaries have arrived! We can't believe our eyes — but it's true. Twelve brand new volumes! There is talk they were sent by the bishop of Fulda.

We would in fact have time to pray from the breviary. But how are we supposed to use a book "without leaving any trace that it has been used?"

After a few bad experiences the books remain in perfect order on the shelf, and we are as bored as before. Later we are permitted to ask for our own breviaries to be sent from home.

+ + +

"Where's the guy from Luxembourg?"

Hugo Gutmann turns up escorting new prisoners. At the same time he tells me that a priest from Luxembourg has arrived in barrack 9. "Don't remember his name." I'm unable to figure out who it is from his description.

And so I wait eagerly to find out who from home will be coming in the next few days to share our suffering. The new prisoner from Luxembourg turns out to be Joseph Knepper, the pastor in Ehleringen. In the first days of July he joins us in the clergy block. We have a good laugh when we welcome him. Knepper is extremely tall and thin, so he appears in trousers that are much too short, a shirt that looks almost short-sleeved on him, and a cap that comes down over his ears. It definitely made up for the tragic aspect of this situation, and certainly my own appearance also contributed to the laughter.

Unfortunately Knepper wasn't assigned to room 3 with me, but to room 4, which was still barely furnished. The prisoners there had to sleep on bare boards, since there weren't enough straw sacks.

After the midday meal we met on the barrack street. It was an uncommonly comforting feeling to hear in my own language how Luxembourg was holding out, and to learn the latest news from the front and what had happened to friends and acquaintances.

+ + +

"Outside, everyone! Take your things with you!"

We pile out into the barrack street. Nobody knows

why. Was somebody caught with a rosary or a picture of a saint again? Or was it the catastrophe that we were expecting hourly, as a result of the strong language the Pope and German bishops had used in their protests?

"Drop everything! Go get the tables, chairs, and beds!"

When the tension has reached a peak we learn the reason for all this: The barrack is going to be re-painted — in dark green. This is because more and more often our nightly sleep is interrupted by the comforting drone of English bombers overhead.

+ + +

The camp has run out of potatoes! Now we have to do without the four or five boiled potatoes we had received up to now with our cabbage or carrot soup.

At the time we thought it was the beginning of the end. Little did we know how much hunger a person can endure.

+ + +

Another new arrival from Luxembourg in the clergy block! This time I succeed in getting him assigned to my room.

It is Pastor Schiltz from Tüntingen. He is wearing a cap that is too tight, so it puffs out at the top like a baker's hat.

All he talks about is his parish — the joys and sor-rows of everyone in his care, "his" children, and before going to sleep he blesses each one individually in his thoughts, with tears in his eyes. I imagine that the Lord is speaking a mighty "Amen" to this blessing.

For my part, I feel like an old-timer at the camp who has to look after the "greenhorn." That gives me a peculiar sense of satisfaction, and renewed courage.

+ + +

Only two days later Schiltz complains of intense pain in one foot. The tried and true prescription in the camp, "just ignore it," proves ineffective. His foot swells up horrifically, and by the time permission finally arrives for him to report to the infirmary, Schiltz collapses after taking a few steps and remains unconscious.

It was an act of providence. He was allowed to spend more than two months in the infirmary "resting."

+ + +

"Who gets the soup that is ladled out of our pail nearly every day?"

"For heaven's sake, pretend you don't notice!" We need many things for our room that can only be obtained by "organizing" them. However "organizing" things is the monopoly of the head prisoners, and they insist on being paid. Today we need oil for the floor. Officially there is no oil, but we will be reported and punished if the floor is not oiled.

+ + +

Bishop Cozal is celebrating the twenty-fifth anniversary of his ordination. He has received permission to say Mass on that day. The Poles are rehearsing what they will sing.

A group of us are constructing a monstrance. We've already acquired the necessary materials: part of a broomstick, some empty tin cans that look like brass on the inside, and several flat pieces of wood. We use the wood to make a multi-level rectangular base and insert the piece of broomstick into the middle for a stem. The bottom of a can becomes a capsule, and we cut the sides artfully to form the rays of a sunburst.

We have spent two weeks working on the monstrance, with only pliers, a hammer, and a table knife for tools. But we succeeded, and we are convinced that the Savior will be as happy to be enthroned there as in one of the costly golden vessels in our churches at home.

+ + +

There are Yugoslavian cigarettes for sale. They are strong and expensive. Dealing in them is a private operation run by the SS divisions who acquire them in newly "liberated" countries and sell them on the black market.

Later there were Bulgarian cigarettes and finally Greek tobacco.

"Don't touch them," a fellow priest who is an old hand advises me. "We're not in good enough shape. Anyone who smokes won't make it through."

+ + +

"Knepper." The name is called out at morning head count. That means the prisoner is being released.

It was early October, not quite three months after

my friend had arrived at the camp. I couldn't even wave good-bye to him, since because he was one of the tallest he was standing several rows behind me.

It's a strange feeling when someone close to you is suddenly released. You are happy for your friend. But as far as you yourself are concerned, you have a sense that luck won't be passing so close to you again for a long time.

Only later did we learn that Knepper had not been freed definitively.

+ + +

Within a few days his replacement arrived. It was Dr. Baptiste Esch — nicknamed "Batty" — an editor at the newspaper *Luxemburger Wort,* who until then had been in Berlin and Camp Sachsenhausen with his supervisor, Monsignor Origer.

When it was time to deliver soup pails I arranged to switch with another priest whose pail was to go to the newcomers' block. That gave me a chance to say a brief "hello" to my friend.

His tone was serious, almost hopeless, as he said, "I won't get out of here alive."

"We'll make it. You'll see." I told him about America and Russia.

"I know we're going to win the war, but I won't ever see home again. Wherever I end up, everything goes wrong."

He spoke without bitterness. A shiver went through me. He was too big a person to make his ordeal easier by indulging in illusions. He would experience every bit of the suffering to the last drop, not only physically, but also mentally. And totally alone. I sensed in that first moment that I would never be able to follow him the entire way.

His prophecy came true. Two weeks later he joined us in the clergy block. And on the very next day the first catastrophe hit us.

The "Good Times"
Come to an End

None of us was ever able to say why the clergy block experienced this catastrophe, or to what it was due. Some people said that the Pope had given a strong speech on the radio, and that the German bishops had issued a public protest. Something must have happened. It was in early October 1941.

It began with the usual shout, "Everybody outside!" We were hustled out into the barrack street. Everyone with the few possessions he was able to grab in haste.

Outside stands the camp commandant in person. Our hearts skip a beat. The other rooms have also lined up in the street. The head prisoners of the rooms and the barracks are rushing around yelling and hitting everyone they can get their hands on. But they don't know what is actually going on either.

They give orders: "Get all your things!" and a moment later, "Leave everything inside!" We expect a "pocket inspection," and while the camp commandant and his staff are dealing with the other barracks we frantically try to get rid of all the forbidden items in them: Rosaries, cigarette ends, toilet paper, rags to wrap our raw feet in . . .

"Germans and Poles line up separately!"

"We're going to be gassed!" screams a Pole next to me who is an ethnic German. He tries to squeeze over into the German ranks.

"Where should the Luxembourgers go?" I ask the head prisoner for the barrack, and get a kick in response. A Dutch Jesuit, Robert Regout, a professor from the University of Nijmegen, calmly joins the ranks of the Poles. Schiltz and I do the same. There we find Batty Esch, too, whom we had momentarily lost from view.

We are herded around like cattle, and when an SS man turns up, he curses and hits out, giving orders and countermanding them, just to make us jumpy and anxious and keep us in motion, so it looks like something is happening. We end up in barrack 28, while another group of us marches on to barrack 30. Simultaneously the Germans who had been assigned to these barracks are moved to barrack 26. For the moment the aim is to separate the German clergymen from those of other nationalities. That this does not mean anything good is clear to all of us.

+ + +

As we stand in front of barrack 28, Camp Commandant Hofmann addresses us.

Dear Reader! To imagine this speech, take the most vulgar expressions you know, and put them in a pot with the greatest nonsense that you have ever heard a human being utter. Add a few insults to the Pope and the Church, lard the whole liberally with "clergy scum" and "pack of priests," and you have a rough approximation of the context in which the only message that really mattered appeared: "The privileges you've had up to now are over."

+ + +

Esch, Schiltz, and I ended up together in room 1. It cost Esch a terrible blow to the head. He had been imprudent enough to ask the new head prisoner for the barrack to allow the three Luxembourgers to stay together. He didn't yet know that the last thing head prisoners could bear was appeals to feelings that they had abandoned completely long ago. He never learned to speak the "camp language." As chance would have it, we nevertheless achieved our goal.

+ + +

More arrivals from Luxembourg for the clergy block. They were Father Joseph Stoffels and Father Nicolas Wampach from the Congregation of the Priests of the Sacred Heart of Jesus, who had been working at the Luxembourg Mission in Paris. Whereas I had come to Dachau directly from Trier, they had spent the previous six months in Buchenwald.

Father Stoffels is a born optimist. Though his poor health may cause him additional physical problems, his wholly unworldly attitude helps him rise above everything else. He is immediately declared unfit for work and does not have to carry food pails.

Father Wampach is a realist and understands well how to adapt. It is touching to see how he constantly looks out for his "boss" and tries to ensure Stoffels' survival along with his own.

+ + +

Both padres joined us in room 1. Now there were five of us sitting at the same table. Today, when I think back and picture my friends, all now deceased, I can hardly believe I didn't ask them more about what they endured before reaching Dachau. Batty Esch told me virtually nothing about his incarceration at Sachsenhausen.

All our thoughts and plans revolved around only one goal: surviving, making it through. We lacked the peace of mind to concentrate on anything else, and hardly spoke at all.

+ + +

The quality of the food declined rapidly. Potatoes became rarities, and the soups grew thinner. Every night meat dishes with lots of fat cropped up in my dreams, but it was sugar and sweet foods that really dominated them. Anyone who has ever spent time in a concentration camp will be familiar with this phenomenon.

Then a wild idea occurred to me. The Poles wrote

their letters on camp stationery, which bore a printed warning in bold type saying they were not allowed to receive packages and that it was pointless to send any. We Luxembourgers, on the other hand, had to use plain white paper. "Who knows?" I said to my friends. "It's possible that if something were mailed to us, they might let us have it. I'm going to risk it."

In my next letter I managed to smuggle the following passage past the censor: "How are my bees doing, and how is the honey harvest this year? It's a shame you can't send me a pot of it."

+ + +

Ten days later I am summoned to an interrogation by the camp commandant himself — a highly unusual occurrence. I was given a fresh shave, including my head, and a clean pair of trousers.

On the way to the commandant I consider very carefully what I am going to say. I have trouble keeping calm. The barrack clerk accompanies me to the administration building; there I take my shoes off, as the regulations require, and stand at attention outside the commandant's door — for three hours.

This time is taken up by an urgent matter. The commandant is seeking to add two more prisoners to the group that looks after his fox terrier, so the head prisoners of the various barracks come and go, to introduce the numerous applicants for the job. Once, when the door is opened, I catch a glimpse of a candidate combing the pooch's hair. He must be doing a bad job of it, though, for a moment later a swift kick sends him flying out. "Too bad," he says as he passes me. "The mutt gets really good food." Finally it's my turn.

"Prisoner 25487, date of birth 8.13.07, reporting, sir!" I announce this at the top of my lungs on entering. If you don't, you're in trouble already.

The commandant ignores me and goes on playing with his dog. I stand at attention and don't move a muscle. Then he picks up a small round package and hurls it at my head. I know better than to react, so I remain completely still and let the object roll along the floor.

"What is that?"

"It must be honey, sir. My mother wrote me that she had sent some." This response had to be shouted in a rapid-fire manner as well.

"What?! Are you out of your mind? Don't you know that's forbidden?"

"Yes, sir. But my mother doesn't, since I'm from Luxembourg and have to write home on plain white stationery."

The commandant is stroking the dog; perhaps this inspires humane thoughts in him.

"Pick it up! Dismissed! Write at once and tell them never to send anything again!"

+ + +

The head prisoner of our room couldn't believe his eyes when I returned in one piece, carrying a parcel. A pot of honey doesn't last long when shared among five men, however.

The whole camp received an order to end our next

letters with the sentence: "We are strictly forbidden to receive any packages."

The new regimen wasn't long in coming. The very next day we were no longer permitted wine, midday rest, or to attend Mass. The German priests didn't come to distribute the big food kettles, so that most of us had to make two trips. Then a new barrier of tangled wire was placed around barrack 26, the German clergy block. That meant we were cut off from the chapel, and when it became evident that we liked to spend the hour when Mass was celebrated lurking near the rear windows of the chapel, they were covered with opaque white paint.

Shortly thereafter our breviaries and rosaries were collected and turned in. Religious activity of any kind was strictly prohibited.

+ + +

"You are now classified as a working block," the barrack head prisoner declared one morning. "That means no one may remain in the day room during working hours except the barrack personnel."

And so from then on we were driven outdoors after morning coffee and had to spend the five hours until it was time to go pick up the food marching, running, singing, and doing "up and down" exercises. It was the same between the midday meal and evening head count — whether it was hot or cold, or pouring rain. The head prisoners would watch us through the windows of the warm day room to make sure none of us pulled up the collars of our thin jackets or stealthily put our hands in our pockets. It was much cosier in the day room when the priests were outside and the privileged gentlemen had it all to themselves.

The head prisoner of barrack 28 was a beast. Unfortunately I have forgotten his name.

+ + +

Work groups are being formed! Anyone who knows a trade or has practical skills is supposed to come forward.

This was the dream of every one of us: to get out of the barrack, to escape the sadistic SS and head prisoners, and to qualify for the "extra ration," which was a sizable piece of bread with margarine or sausage handed out to prisoners on work detail during the morning.

Anyone who was strong enough and could plausibly claim any kind of skill signed up. I listed half a dozen right away. Nothing came of it, however. The camp authorities were still reluctant to let us mix with the other prisoners.

Winter Approaches

The first snow fell on the feast of All Saints. It filled us with alarm, since we had already learned what that meant for the clergy from the old hands in the camp. And sure enough, right after morning head count came the order: "The clergy report to shovel snow!"

We are given boards for scraping, shovels, and wheelbarrows. There are about 200 of the last named, apparently solely for this purpose.

The work had to be done at a jogging pace — so the sun wouldn't melt the few centimeters of snow by itself and spoil all the fun. This time heaven was on our side, though; we had hardly got started when the sun completed its act of mercy.

+ + +

On November 15 winter clothing is issued. This means that our cotton suits are exchanged for ones

made of thicker material. Word goes around that soon
we will get coats and socks in addition. The previous
winter there were even gloves. The next time snow fell
we did indeed have gloves — but no coats or socks.

The fact remained: Toughening up and getting used
to the cold was the best overcoat, and we had already
acquired a thick layer of that kind of protection.

+ + +

Another new arrival from Luxembourg for the
clergy block: Pastor Jean Brachmond from Moersdorf.

He was already a legendary figure, known to all of us
by reputation. Everyone had a story to tell about the
tricks he had played on the Germans. We were looking
forward to hearing confirmation of them from the
source.

For the time being he remained in the new prisoners' barrack, and I had only one opportunity to say a
brief hello to him there.

+ + +

Father Stoffels came down with a kind of inflam-
matory skin rash that soon covered his entire face. It
was the luckiest thing that could have happened to
him, since it was contagious and he was immediately
sent to the infirmary and remained there for months.
At that time prisoners still received decent care.

Despite being kept in strict isolation, he often
managed to send us little messages that bore witness
to his rich spiritual life. They became our devotional
reading.

The sender paid the "postage fee" with his bread ration.

+ + +

As we are exercising, the head prisoner of the whole camp suddenly appears: "Everyone back to the barracks! Get your things and fall in again here!" The order gives rise to the usual agitation, fear, and total confusion.

We are being moved to barrack 30, to share quarters with the clergy already housed there. That means that occupants of two already crowded blocks — roughly 700 men — are jammed into this one miserable space.

Schiltz lands in room 2, while Esch, Wampach, and I are assigned to room 1. Once the initial uproar died down, we wanted to try to move together again, to the room with the best head prisoner. We never managed it. Brachmond ended up joining Schiltz in room 2, and on his release from the infirmary Father Stoffels was sent to room 4.

+ + +

The day rooms and bunk rooms in the overcrowded barrack 30 present a picture of complete chaos. Bunks are put up in the day room and lockers in the sleeping quarters. There are two beds for five men. Esch and I capture a straw mattress for the two of us, however, and succeed in keeping our claim on it for the whole time.

We eat sitting on the floor or on the beds, even though there is not enough head room above the bunks to sit upright. Nevertheless something good results from this: The insane rules about making beds are no longer enforced, and the inspections come to an end. In other ways, too, maintaining strict discipline about housekeeping in the barrack has become an impossibility.

Each of us has only two thin blankets, and the weather has turned bitterly cold. So we first roll up in one blanket and lay the two others over us both.

+ + +

A letter for me! Every letter was a source of consolation and joy. This time, however, the entire content consisted of a scrap of paper with the single sentence, "The use of envelopes with linings is forbidden."

+ + +

"Fall in outside!" The head prisoner of the barrack shouts this order from the door.

We are in the midst of our midday meal. Everyone leaps to his feet, except for someone next to me, who breaks down. He is weeping from overwrought nerves, hunger, and fatigue. I pull him to his feet and press his cap into his hand.

A few minutes later the occupants of the four rooms have just formed up in rows of ten, when the camp commandant strides around the corner of the barrack.

"Attention!"

We stand at attention as if made of stone. This annoys the man, who wants to yell and rant at us but can't find anything to criticize.

"I told you before that there are to be no more privileges for you. Only the German priests will continue to receive special treatment. Are there any Germans still here?"

No one moves.

"Are any of you ethnic Germans?"

The temptation is terrible. It conjures up visions of a warm day room in barrack 26. We imagine the peace and quiet there, and the chapel.

"For the last time: Ethnic Germans come forward!"

An interpreter repeats the order in Polish. The silence is eerie.

Someone behind me clutches my hand. "Absolutely not!" whispers Batty Esch. His is so agitated his voice is shaking.

An ethnic German from Poland steps forward. His name is taken down. In the three weeks that it takes until he is actually transferred to block 26, no one speaks to him.

The commandant confers with his adjutant.

"Luxembourgers come forward!"

Now we have to identify ourselves. I am called into the barrack to speak to the adjutant and give him our six names.

"Are you ethnic Germans?"

"We are treated as such," I reply, congratulating myself on my diplomatic phrasing.

But the fellow has seen through me.

"Dismissed!" That is as good as a death sentence.

The two executioners vanish along the same path by which they had arrived. When we return to our soup it is cold.

+ + +

We hear that eighteen men are to be chosen for a work detail. Nobody has any idea what sort of work it will involve. Esch and I volunteer immediately, thinking of the extra ration and a chance to spend some time indoors.

In a column of more than 50 men we march to barrack 2, where the labor office is located. There we are examined. Esch is chosen, I am rejected. I return to our block, richer by a few kicks.

From now on Esch belongs to "Transport Commando 2," also known as "the Marsh Express." The transport concerned is a trailer for a heavy truck, mounted on inflated tires and pulled by eighteen prisoners. Two men pull a shaft at the front, four push from the rear, and six men on each side pull in pairs in harnesses that are attached to the sides of the trailer by wire cables. There are half a dozen such trailers, used to ferry all sorts of loads to and from the camp, the supply depot, and the train station of the "SS town."

After this I see Batty Esch only at meals and in the evening, when he collapses onto our straw mattress, exhausted.

"It's too late for us," he says then, or words to that effect. "We're already too weak to work. The extra ration doesn't make up for the increased effort we have to exert."

+ + +

The ground is icy.

As we dash out into the pitch blackness to go get the morning coffee, we go sprawling headlong, one after the other. Our wooden clogs don't have any grip on the ice.

Marching is torture in itself. If in addition we have to carry the heavy, brimming pails, we have no chance at all.

Then someone shows us how to do it: He takes off his clogs and walks barefoot on the ice. My partner and I do the same — and then the task becomes possible.

Our room is heated for the first time. The huge tiled stove does its best, but there is a shortage of fuel, and a few briquettes have to be saved for the evening, so that the barrack head prisoner and those of the various rooms can fry the potatoes they've withheld from our ration in the grease they've also withheld.

Nevertheless it feels good to come into the room out of the cold, which is already severe for the time of year. If the head prisoner is out, or if he's asleep, one can even dare to lean against the stove, or put a wet jacket on it to dry.

+ + +

Coats and socks are handed out. The former are striped, the latter speckled and multi-colored. Hardly any of the original wool remains visible. It is almost entirely covered by the various patches of cloth that the owner, depending on his organizing talent, had been able to acquire and sew on. "As thick as possible" is the watchword.

Nevertheless both coats and socks provide measurable relief from the cold.

+ + +

I have scalded my hands while carrying food pails. The burn looks bad and hurts twice as much in the cold.

I am allowed to go to the infirmary to have it bandaged. There I look around, hoping to run into my friend J. Elsen, who has already given me many bandages along with occasional news about the other prisoners from Luxembourg.

He's not there; it turns out he was released months ago. That means he's certainly been to visit my mother and given her my love.

The person I barely manage to avoid running into, on the other hand, is Dr. Heiden, the head of the infirmary. Although he's a prisoner himself, he is a brute who has as many people on his conscience as some of the SS men.

+ + +

I am on punishment detail. There were a few crumbs of bread in my locker, so I am a dirty pig, a piece of filth.

Consequently I am ordered to join the work detail headed for "Eyke Square." That is the name of a fairly large open space at the end of a broad avenue in the SS town, where the high-ranking officers have their villas.

Our job is to wield our brooms and load the sweepings onto a little cart. An SS man accompanies us, since the site is outside the camp walls.

A woman comes toward us, leading a child by the hand. The encounter seems to me like an apparition from another world. She is the first "civilian" life form I have laid eyes on in six months.

I wonder what she may be thinking. Does she know about our misery? Does she really consider us criminals? Or feel any empathy for us at all?

And what about the child?

The two of them are free. Can go wherever they want. Probably they are on their way to a comfortable home, where they will spend Sunday afternoon with daddy, who has today off. He is an SS man and earns a good salary . . .

The SS guard rouses me from my daydream with a poke in the ribs. "That's the wife of the camp commandant. *She's* allowed to keep her fur coat. *My* wife had to donate her rabbit fur to the clothing drive for soldiers on the eastern front."

+ + +

It's Sunday. Esch, Wampach, and I quietly slip out of the clergy block and mingle with the other prisoners who are walking up and down on the main camp road. We drift toward the newcomers' block without drawing attention to ourselves. For days we have been seeking an opportunity to say hello to Jis Thorn, a lawyer who arrived on November 25.

Someone goes to tell him we are waiting by the barbed-wire fence. He stands straight and tall. We envy him, for he is still in good shape.

He doesn't say much, but he is full of optimism. That is enough for us for the moment. When he is moved out of the newcomers' barrack we will see him more often.

+ + +

"The English have recaptured Tobruk," reports Batty Esch when he returns from work. "An SS man told us."

I am overjoyed and rush to tell Wampach, Brachmond, Schiltz, and Stoffels. Brachmond comes back with me. "It will go quickly now, you'll see." He is quite excited and has also heard lots of rumors about the eastern front again.

"Nonsense," is Batty's only comment.

+ + +

"You're letting things get you down," I say to Esch that evening when we are lying on our straw mattress. "No," he replies, "but I *won't* talk myself into believing the impossible. Tobruk may fall, but the war won't be over all that soon. I don't want to sugar-coat the suffering with fairy tales for children."

I feel nervous, for I sense that I need such "fairy tales" in order to keep up my courage. My friend's bleak attitude would be toxic and destructive for me — and will be for him, too, even though he won't admit it.

"You don't get along with anyone. It's your own fault if people are turning their backs on you. We *want* to cling to every straw! Every bit of hope is welcome, if it helps me to keep going and feel strong inside, even if the image is a false one, a mirage. You want to play the part of a hero, a tough guy, but you're only making yourself depressed and robbing the rest of us of hope at the same time . . . "

I was exhausted and close to despair. I meant what I had said, every word of it. I was too miserable to express my thoughts less baldly, with more consideration for his feelings.

"So I'm all alone now," said Batty Esch.

I said nothing. We both sensed how a wall was descending and dividing us. Unavoidably, since we hadn't the strength to surmount it.

I can truly say that, psychologically and emotionally, this moment was one of the hardest I experienced in all my time at the camp.

Neither of us was able to sleep.

I wept, and I believe he did the same. Was it minutes or hours that went by like this?

Then suddenly, after an involuntary movement, he was holding my hand in his. He gripped it firmly, and I returned the pressure.

"Let's stick together!" Batty whispered.

"Yes," was all I said.

And then we fell asleep, happy.

Christmas 1941

Christmas Eve in the concentration camp!

We are allowed to stay up later than usual. From somewhere a pine bough has suddenly appeared. It is stuck in a tin can and decorated with two candles, which we light. Someone made them using his margarine ration from Thursday. Then the Poles sing melancholy songs.

A man with a marvelous voice sings the *Gloria* to the tune of an old chorale. *Et in terra pax hominibus* . . . The Polish bishop gives a commentary. I don't understand much of it. May our sacrifice contribute to bringing peace to the world.

The head prisoner starts to find all this boring. He goes and gets his colleagues from the other rooms, and they all sing *O du lieber Augustin*.

We go to bed feeling sad and dream of home.

+ + +

"I'm on gate duty today," Cappy whispers to me. We are returning from the assembly square on Christmas morning, and our column is marching alongside the German clergy's column for a brief moment.

When it is time to deliver the pails for the midday meal I exchange with a colleague assigned to go to barrack 26 that day. I suspect that Cappy wants to give me something and am eager to find out what it is.

He is standing at the entrance of the barbed-wire barrier around the barrack, as announced. We are not allowed to enter, but have to leave the pails in front of the "gate." I set mine down next to Cappy, and as he bends down to pick it up he quickly presses a carefully folded piece of paper into my hand. Very softly he mouths the word *"ichthys."*

I have difficulty concealing my excitement. Swiftly I hide the precious gift in my glove. And as I hurry back home images from the time of the catacombs come to mind. Back then, as now, the Most Holy had to be preserved from desecration, and so the Greek term for "fish," *ichthys*, became a code word for the Eucharist, since it is composed of the initial letters of the phrase "Jesus Christ, Son of God, Savior."

After the evening meal we Luxembourgers met a few friends inconspicuously in the darkness outside the barrack and divided the precious pieces into as many particles as humanly possible. And then the Christ Child entered our hearts . . .

+ + +

A few days later a transport of 600 Polish priests arrives.

As we go to get the midday food pails they are standing in the assembly square, some of them still in their own clothes, the others already in prisoners' uniforms, shivering in the bitter cold.

When we assemble for the evening head count they are still there. They are given only summer uniforms, without caps or coats. Desperately they rub their bare heads, which have just been shaved.

Word goes round that a dozen or more have already collapsed. They are all older men, the entire remaining clergy of a diocese in which the younger priests were arrested earlier. One of the occupants of our room recognizes his pastor and starts to sob.

The entire group is housed in block 28; their expected arrival was the reason why we had to move out.

Within six weeks a third of the new arrivals are already dead.

+ + +

On Sunday there is pureed pea soup. Apart from the bread ration it is the only truly nourishing meal we get during the entire week. The head prisoner of our room has chosen today to inspect our eating utensils. Father Wampach's mess-tin fails to pass muster and remains empty. I spill a drop of soup on the floor. At once the beast rips the tin out of my hands and pours its contents back into the pail.

After the meal is over he sends a full pail of lovely soup to his fellows. Wampach and I cried like little children.

+ + +

The first days of January 1942 brought enormous amounts of snow. The reader already knows what snow meant for the clergy. But this time the torture surpassed the bounds of the endurable. At the same time the thermometer hovered between 5 and 15 degrees below zero. From morning till night we scraped, shoveled, and pushed wheelbarrow after wheelbarrow of snow to the brook. The work detail consisted of more than 1,000 clergymen, forced to keep moving by SS men and Capos who kicked us and beat us with truncheons.

We had to make rounds with the wheelbarrows from the assembly square to the brook and back. Not a moment of rest was allowed, and much of the time we were forced to run.

At one point I tripped over my barrow and fell, and it took me a while to get up again. An SS man dashed over and ordered me to run with the full load. He ran beside me, beating me constantly with a leather strap. When I got to the brook I was not allowed to dump out the heavy snow, but had to make a second complete round with it instead.

When the guard finally went off and I tried to let go of the wheelbarrow, I found that one of my hands was frozen fast to it. I had to blow on it with my warm breath to get it free.

+ + +

There weren't enough wheelbarrows available. Some of us were ordered to fetch the table tops from the day rooms of our barracks. We piled up the snow on them and then four men carried each one on their shoulders.

+ + +

In great haste a double barrier of tangled wire was erected around barracks 25, 27, and 29. The whole block is intended for Russian prisoners of war. The matter is so urgent that the work goes on day and night. Then the barracks stand empty for three months.

When the Russians finally arrived — 300 officers, we heard — it was for barely six weeks. After that they were taken away from the camp and never seen again. The next day we were given 300 Russian uniforms to disinfect and cut into strips for the wartime textile collection.

+ + +

The camp canteen has canned peas!

The priests are not allowed any.

But Jennes has a solution. He has no money left in his account. We contribute, and he faithfully brings us some of the cans he has bought — in complete secrecy, since this is dangerous both for him and for us.

All I know about Jennes is his name and the fact that he was a loyal soul who did a number of favors in Dachau for the priests from Luxembourg.

Perhaps he is still alive and may read these lines. And pay me a visit.

+ + +

Word reaches us that our compatriot Franz Clément has arrived, a prominent socialist politician and writer. We agree to risk a visit to the newcomers' barrack on the following Sunday afternoon. Batty Esch draws Sunday duty, however, and the others are afraid. So I wind up going by myself.

I find Franz Clément altered almost beyond recognition. He looks terrible. He grasps my hand and presses it firmly. "Where is Batty Esch?" he asks.

"He would have come along, but he was assigned to work detail."

"Tell him that I am looking forward to shaking his hand."

I return to our block in high spirits.

+ + +

A week later we go back: Esch, Brachmond, and I. Clément walked straight up to Esch, gripped his broad shoulders and embraced him.

"Let's forget what happened in the past! I was wrong. It turns out that the ones who hold out and behave best are you padres . . ."

Esch couldn't get a single word out. He was crying like a child.

Ten Days' Leave and
My Return to Dachau

February 6. I have been incarcerated for a year. It seems terribly long and amazingly short. I do not indulge any foolish hopes. Nevertheless I have to force myself to remain calm on the way to the morning head count. Maybe my sentence is limited.

My heart is pounding when, after we've been counted, the camp runner comes toward our column with a piece of paper in his hand. He passes by us, however, and two unknown names from the neighboring barrack are called out . . .

+ + +

February 11. During the morning head count a name is suddenly announced: Schiltz, Michel! I see motion a few rows in front of me. Then my friend Schiltz comes past looking dazed and takes his place with the other lucky ones at the back of the column. I don't dare even to turn my head.

Later, when we go to get the midday food pails, Schiltz is standing near the kitchen waiting to depart. I am able to wave to him furtively. But how many unspoken thoughts were conveyed by that gesture!

+ + +

Sunday, February 15. There is pea soup at midday. It is a consolation that helps us forget many things, including the insidious snowflakes that tumble down occasionally from a heavily overcast sky. For weeks the snow has been at least a foot deep, but it is so packed down and icy that we are waiting for a fresh snowfall to be able to shovel again . . .

+ + +

I have just got my bowl of soup and taken the first spoonful, hunched on the bunk next to Esch, when the door flies open. "Attention!" We leap to our feet.

"25487! You must come with me immediately!"

"You're being released!" someone whispers.

I hand Batty my soup and reach mechanically for my cap, coat, and clogs. There isn't time for a handshake. The SS man is already shouting, "Step on it!"

As I am going out the door I just catch the last thing Batty calls after me: "Tre'scht meng Mamm!" ["Comfort my Mom."]

+ + +

And then I walk, slide, and stumble along beside the SS man through the deep snow and ice to the administration building. We don't go by way of the broad main camp street but around the back of the barrack. I have to take off my wooden clogs in order to keep up with him.

He doesn't look particularly nasty, so I risk a question: "What is this about?"

"Don't know. You're going to see the commandant himself. Must be release." All the same I don't feel happy, but rather terribly nervous. No one is ever released on a Sunday. And certainly not in the middle of the day.

+ + +

At commandant's office things moved quickly.

"How much money do you have?"

"Thirty marks."

"Is that enough to get to Luxembourg?"

"Yes, it is," I say and can hardly contain myself for excitement.

"Get ready! In ten minutes I want you out of here!"

And then he personally accompanied me to the place where all the prisoners' clothes were stored, which was always closed on Sundays.

I did everything as if in a dream. I could feel that something wasn't quite right.

The commandant helped me into my trousers . . . Had the world gone mad?

It's impossible for me put my shoes on, however. My feet have swollen into shapeless masses from going barefoot, from infected cuts and chilblains. But I recall that I have slippers. With difficulty I manage to put them on.

And in only a little more than ten minutes I am actually walking toward the exit.

+ + +

"You'll get your papers at the gate," says the SS man accompanying me.

In the entryway he exchanges a few words with the guard. Then I am handed a form on which is printed: *Notification of Release*. The word *Release* has been crossed out, however, and replaced with *10 Days' Leave*.

I am in a state of shock and stare at the piece of paper, on the verge of breaking down completely.

At that moment the door of the guards' room flies open and a nasty mouth spits out the words, "Why are you standing around like a total idiot, rev? Go home and bury your mother, stupid!"

This was how I learned that my mother had died.

+ + +

Then I am standing outside and staring at the paper in my hand. And feeling as if everything must be falling apart.

My SS guard pokes me. "*My* mother has been dead for a long time . . . I'm supposed to go to the station with you . . . but I think you'll be able to find the way by yourself . . ."

"Thanks," is all I say.

And remain standing there, in my slippers, in the snow. With my suitcase in one hand and the notification in the other. The whole world is spinning.

How long I stood like that, with the world in front

of me and the closed gate to the camp behind me, I don't know.

An SS officer who was approaching the gate brought me abruptly back to reality. I gripped my suitcase harder and began walking. As I passed the man all my muscles twitched as if to carry out the commands "Attention!" and "Cap off!" I caught myself in the nick of time and insolently looked him right in the face as we came abreast.

And then I am following the road. The area is totally unfamiliar to me, since when I passed along here going in the opposite direction ten months earlier I was in a hermetically sealed prison van. In my thoughts I am with my mother. When did she die? Has she already been buried? And what is the meaning of this leave? Such a thing has never happened before in the whole history of the camp!

+ + +

Despite the icy cold I have to take off my coat. I can't tolerate so many layers of clothing any more. The snow is so dry that I manage quite well in my slippers. When I reach the first houses of the little town of Dachau I ask the way to the railroad station. The man gazes after me for a long while. Only now do I notice that I am attracting the notice of everybody going by. My cassock and clerical hat are probably the cause.

In some glances I believe I detect empathy and pity.

+ + +

At the station I learn that I have a good hour until the next train to Munich.

At the same time I suddenly notice a ravenous feeling of hunger. "Just go to the kitchen," the owner of the station restaurant says when I explain to him that I have no ration stamps.

A short time later he follows me, and when he sees my shaved head he serves me gigantic portions of soup and potatoes. The specialty of the house: once, twice, and so on until the train whistles that it is ready to depart.

+ + +

In Munich I have to wait again for three hours.

I make a beeline for the restaurant and immediately order the "specialty of the house." After the second serving I have to stop, since it is half-past two and after that time they are not allowed to serve hot food anymore.

On the advice of the waitress I go across the street to a pastry shop. She even gives me some ration stamps for bread, for which I can get several pieces of cake.

Only now does it occur to me that my best course of action would have been to go directly to the nearest rectory or monastery. I make inquiries and end up with the Augustinian Fathers, who welcome me with open arms. I am able to wash and find myself sitting once more at a table laden with food.

The Father Superior leaves me alone for a moment, and I seize the opportunity to polish off half the loaf of bread in front of me.

"But brother, you didn't bring any bread for the

Lord!" I say nothing and simply eat the other half of the loaf, too.

+ + +

When I am on my way to the train station again I feel much stronger.

I let myself be swept past the barrier by the stream of people and turn out to be standing in front of an express train for Lindau on the Lake of Constance.

All of a sudden a thought flashes through my mind: What if everything I have been told weren't true? Maybe my mother isn't dead at all, and my sisters or some powerful friend have made up the whole story in order to offer me an opportunity to escape? An insane feeling of hope overcomes me.

I drift casually past the cars just to gain some time for reflection. Am I being observed? I am terribly conspicuous in my cassock and Roman hat, but all the same I don't have the impression that anyone is keeping me under surveillance.

I know Lindau and the Lake of Constance well. I even have friends there. A few days to recover in some rectory and then escape to Switzerland in the dark of night in a rowboat or with a life jacket! . . .

But then I recall more calmly that my mother's death must be a matter of official record. And besides, being granted this leave is so exceptional that someone certainly had to vouch personally for my return.

And so I boarded the train that took me home.

The long journey passed like a dream. My mind was completely devoid of thoughts. And it didn't matter a bit that everyone in the crowded train was looking at me.

+ + +

Not until I reached home and hugged my brothers and sisters was the spell broken. Then I cried my eyes out.

I had to go to the cemetery to say good-bye to my mother. Her loyal heart had been forced to endure too much suffering and distress. Some days before people from the Gestapo had made a nasty scene. It was too much for her. She gave her life to save mine.

+ + +

Then I had to follow my orders and report to the Villa Pauly, the Gestapo headquarters.

"How are you doing?" inquired Friedrichs, the secretary of the criminal police.

"Well."

"Do you have enough to eat there?"

"No."

"Are you beaten?"

"Yes."

"How are your colleagues? Have they had enough? Don't they want to come home?"

I suddenly realize what he is getting at. It would be a great propaganda success: Six Luxembourg clergymen return home after being "re-educated" at Dachau. Was *this* the explanation for my unheard-of leave?

Was it possible that, for a moment, I held the lives of my friends in my hand?

"Well, how is it? Have the gentlemen's attitudes softened up a bit in the meantime?"

In my mind's eye I see my friends: miserable, cold, and hungry. At the same time, however, a face appears before me, as if carved in stone, teeth gritted, with an ambivalent expression, revealing both unspeakable suffering and at the same time an infinite, almost mocking contempt. This was the mask that Batty Esch wore every day in the camp.

"You'll have to ask them yourself," I replied.

It took a moment for the Gestapo man to digest his defeat. Then he spoke in a honeyed tone: "You yourself will certainly be released soon. If you have to go back, it won't be for long."

That was the silken thread with which the Gestapo kept me more firmly bound than a guard posted in front of my family's house could have done.

+ + +

The following day I had the good fortune to stand at the altar again. For the first time in ten months.

Otherwise the leave passed quickly.

+ + +

On February 25 a train took me toward the misery of the camp again. I will not describe here what my feelings were.

It was good I had no inkling that the real hell was only about to begin.

During the trip the thought of fleeing crossed my mind again and again.

It was out of the question though. In Paris my
brother had provided a guarantee that I would return,
and what was it that Friedrichs had said to me as I left
the Villa Pauly: "You come from a large family, don't
you?" That was clear enough.

So I gritted my teeth and was standing at the camp
gate, as my orders stated, on February 25 at 5 p.m. on
the dot, after choking down three hard-boiled eggs.

"Reporting back from leave," I say.

The man is so amazed that he stands there for a
moment open-mouthed before he scuttles away to
get instructions . . .

+ + +

The formalities are taken care of rapidly.

When I turn in my civilian possessions I hold two
things under the SS guard's nose: a huge ham sandwich and a pack of Dutch cigarillos.

The man understands immediately. He looks
around once quickly, then slides the cigarillos into his
pocket, while I am allowed to keep the sandwich to
give to Batty Esch. Getting outfitted with a new uniform is annoying, because over the months I had altered the parts of my old one to fit better; now they
are gone and I have to start all over again with an impossible set, like a pathetic newcomer.

+ + +

My friends can't get over their amazement, since they
thought I had been released for good . . . Luckily I get my
old place back, with Batty Esch in barrack 30, room 1.

Batty retreats at once into a corner with the ham sandwich and doesn't come back until the very last crumb has disappeared.

+ + +

That evening we gather in the barrack street and I have to tell them about home, about how vile the Nazis' behavior has been and how stubbornly people in Luxembourg have resisted them; I talk about how the war is going and about crazy hopes. I had stuffed myself full of everything that could offer comfort and make them optimistic.

For my part I learn that Representative Weyrich has died in the camp in the meantime. Some one has heard it was supposedly during a lung operation. They tell me further that Franz Clément is suffering from terrible eczema covering his whole head. That Father Wampach has moved into room 4 with Father Stoffels.

And that starting next month all prisoners who are not already doing other work will be assigned to the "plantation."

+ + +

The "plantation" is every prisoner's worst fear, a huge cultivated area that has been progressively wrested from the marshy Dachau land at the cost of countless human lives. It is crisscrossed with paths and is used chiefly for growing medicinal plants.

Working on the plantation doesn't count as "labor," rather it is a way to "utilize" prisoners who are unfit for anything else. Accordingly those who work there receive no extra ration.

In reality the plantation's acres are killing fields. Whatever the weather, the prisoners have to perform all tasks by hand, hundreds of them on their knees pulling up weeds, crawling around in ditches full of water with a pestilential stench, without any possibility of finding shelter — either from the wind and rain or from the capos, who treat them like cattle.

The goal is to avoid the plantation at all costs. That means getting assigned to a "proper" work detail, perhaps related to a craft or trade, one that works indoors and receives the extra ration.

Batty Esch still belongs to "transport commando #2." In other words he's not under a roof, but it's better than the plantation, and its members get the additional food. He has already set wheels in motion to try to procure a similar job for me.

+ + +

In the last days of February the guards can celebrate orgies of "snow sadism."

It snows without letup. We scrape and shovel, push and carry loads of snow until some of the priests pass out from exhaustion.

From his window above the entryway the camp commandant watches the merry-go-round at his feet with visible pleasure. From time to time he sends a camp runner down to the capos: Tempo, tempo! Beat them more if you have to!

And then we pick up the wheelbarrows and the

table tops piled with snow and run another race with death. It is deliverance when the whistle finally blows to go carry the food pails.

"Transport Commando Praezifix"

I had to carry my pail a long way and was one of the last to return to the barrack, dead tired.

As I reach the door the camp capo pushes his way in beside me and shouts: "Seventeen men fall in, right now!"

I think it over. Seventeen men, that certainly means labor outside the camp. I'm back outside in a flash and the first one standing "in formation."

"Let's go!"

We march to the labor office. While they are looking us over I clench my teeth, stand stiffly at attention and suppress my tiredness. I manage to be one of the chosen group, and we are informed that from now on we will be known as the "Transport Commando Praezifix."

A chill runs down my spine. "Praezifix" is one of the hardest assignments. Nevertheless I'm happy, since the members of the commando get more to eat.

Right away they give us real shoes with thick wooden soles, and better coats, caps, and gloves. We are introduced to our capo and ordered to report to our wagon the following day after the morning tally.

+ + +

I can hardly sleep for excitement. Now I will be removed from constant torment by the head prisoners in the barrack. I simply won't be there anymore when lockers are inspected, when the order is given to shovel snow or deliver barrows of coal, or it's time to carry food pails. At midday we will eat outside the camp. I'll be able to get a glimpse of places outside the walls once again. And there will be enough to eat!

The Praezifix wagon turns out to be exactly like the one on which Batty Esch earns his bread: a heavy truck trailer mounted on inflated tires, with a shaft attached at the front. On both sides three wire cables are attached, each one connected to a harness for two men. Two men pull from the front and steer with the shaft, the remaining four push from the rear.

Right after the morning head count, at 5:30 a.m., we race to the wagon, which stands next to the kitchen, hitch ourselves up, and are off at a gallop to the front of the camp. There the various commandos are called out, with and without their wagons; they are counted and their assignments are noted. They receive the appropriate number of SS guards for their task and disappear through the gate.

We are given three heavily armed SS men to accompany us on our way.

Our wagon is empty. Or no, not completely; we are hauling with us the most important thing of all, a welcome load: the box of bread on which all our longing is concentrated.

+ + +

Our task is twofold: We are to haul the soup pails from the camp kitchen to the various external commandos or work crews who eat their midday meal outside the camp, and then we will bring the empty pails back to the kitchen. For the time in between, however, we and our vehicle are at the disposition of the "Praezifix" factory in Dachau, which makes screws. We do some clean-up duty there, but our main job is to transport machines and material from the "old factory" in the town of Dachau itself to the "new factory" that is being built on the outskirts. For the eighteen men, plus three SS guards, plus the wagon, the factory pays the camp a grand total of 2 marks and 40 pfennigs per day. That is the value attached to our labor . . .

All this is related to us as we go by the capo, a prisoner himself, it should be understood, but not a priest. The former Praezifix commando was disbanded after complaints from the men in charge at the factory, who announced that in the future they would be willing to work only with priests. Well, that was gratifying in its own way, we thought . . .

My first day as a member of the "Transport Commando Praezifix" is March 19, the feast of St. Joseph. I say a prayer to him as we roll the wagon out of the gate.

My place is on the right side of the wagon, where I

pull on the same cable as a young Polish priest from Warsaw named Stani Suske. We are of the same height and same strength, an important factor in being harnessed together. He speaks some French, and so we can carry on a fine conversation under the noses of the capo and the guards.

On the level road the wagon moves relatively easily. But soon our feet start to hurt. They are swollen from going barefoot and from water retention, and unaccustomed to the stiff, heavy shoes. By evening we will have rubbed all the skin on our feet raw. Still it is relief not to have to curl one's toes with every step, as was necessary to keep from losing the clogs.

The cold has given way to a thaw. The middle of the road is free of snow, but the "draft horses" on the sides of the wagon have to wade through melting snow and water at the edges.

We speak little. Every man is occupied with his own thoughts. Will he be able to hold up? And how much will there be to eat?

After twenty minutes' progress we reach the first houses of Dachau. Soon we turn off to the left and follow a small path between gardens. We run at a gallop in order not to get stuck in snow and mud, but this means that at the same time we are always in danger of being crushed against a wall by the lurching and swaying wagon.

Finally we have arrived at Praezifix. We roll through an iron gate into the rather large factory yard. The capo disappears into the administration building and returns with the chief engineer of the SS.

"All priests?"

"Yes, sir, chief engineer!" The impression we make seems to be more favorable than not. Then the chief starts discussing the day's assignment with the capo.

+ + +

By now it must be about 7 a.m. The factory is already in high gear.

With two others I am ordered onto the factory floor, where we stand around between the lathes and collect and carry out the iron shavings. There is a broom not far from us leaning against the wall, but we don't dare to go get it, so we scrape the shavings together with our hands. We have to be careful, since they are incredibly sharp.

Our mates outside are shoveling coal and cleaning up.

Suske has captured the best job: His assignment is to see to the central heating in the chief's villa, and he is sitting there dry and warm, without anyone watching over him.

After less than an hour a whistle signals us to assemble again. We are supposed to go to the train station. And what are we taking to the station? A package of screws about the size of two cigar boxes.

In our innocence we ask ourselves why this requires eighteen men plus three guards plus a five-ton trailer . . . We haven't yet learned that prisoners, guards, and wagon are never allowed to split up. That is the first law of all external work details . . .

And so we pull the heavy wagon with the little

package through the muddy road to the station and back again. Gradually we break ourselves of the habit of thinking.

+ + +

About nine thirty it's time for a break: the extra ration!

In a flash we are gathered around the promising bread box. The slices of bread are prepared and counted. They are quite a decent-sized portion, and each of us gets a piece of liverwurst, too.

"Twice a week there's margarine," says the capo. We sit down on a pile of coal. I don't think anything has ever tasted better in my life.

I feel completely transformed and am suddenly convinced that I can carry the world on my shoulders.

Toward ten thirty we hitch ourselves up again and set out for the camp.

At the kitchen we load the soup pails for half a dozen external work crews along with our own pail. A quick glance at the latter indicates that it is about half full. It's only turnip soup, but still there are 25 quarts of it for 18 men. Our hearts leap for joy.

The wagon is heavy, however. And we have to be careful that too much doesn't spill out of the brimming pails, for otherwise when we deliver them the capos of the other commandos will beat us.

+ + +

Our route takes us on marshy lanes through the whole area surrounding the camp.

Finally, dead tired, we end up at the "New Praezifix," where we eat our own meal. Getting our bowls and spoons from the wagon, we make ourselves comfortable in some kind of shed. There are in fact about three pints for each of us, and even if it's mostly water, it fills us up.

The guards have their own food, and it's good quality. What they have left over they give to the capo.

They do that for good reason, since it's not the guards who are in command of the expedition, but the capo. The guards have to accompany the wagon to the place where the capo orders us to go. The less we work and the less we run, the less they have to keep up with us. But if the capo slacks off too much, he risks being reported or even removed from his job, so he has the guards pay him with meat and potatoes for taking this risk.

+ + +

Someone wants to take off his shoes.

"Absolutely not," advises the capo, "otherwise you won't be able to keep up afterwards."

He was right. I learned this from experience myself later on.

After our meal we receive an order by telephone to get a load of sand from the gravel pit for the "Old Praezifix" factory.

We go through the whole SS area again and then set out cross-country on dirt tracks between fields. A commando of strong prisoners works in the gravel pit. We are given shovels and start loading. It isn't easy, since we are standing in a hollow and have to throw every shovelful a long way up to the wagon.

A fellow crew member starts to weep. "It's impossible, we're not up to anything any more. It's too late for us."

I don't want to admit it and start shoveling faster in a rage.

+ + +

At the "Old Praezifix" we unload the sand and then do some less strenuous work in the factory, finally setting out for home at about five.

We make the same round as in the morning, picking up the empty pails from the various work crews and finally reach the assembly yard at a gallop, where everyone else has been standing in formation for a long time, ready for the evening head count.

+ + +

Afterwards the capo is waiting for us at the infirmary. He knows the head attendant there and has him bandage our feet.

They look ghastly. Our socks are revolting: filthy and so soaked with blood that they stick to the open wounds.

"You'll have to get used to it," says the capo. "I can use only good runners. You have to reckon with up to 18 kilometers a day . . ."

Thanks to the capo's buddy we are given fairly good treatment; he swathes our feet in layer upon layer of adhesive bandages.

Only one crew member got a box on the ear because he flinched when the attendant ripped the sock off his foot.

When I dropped on my straw mattress that first evening, I felt as if I would never wake up again.

+ + +

And so the first days passed in the Transport Commando Praezifix. Gradually we got used to the shoes and the running. For the rest, a good spirit of comradeship prevailed among the eighteen men, and compared with his fellows, the capo was a decent human being.

If someone collapsed, he was laid on the wagon until he recovered. We left the four "pushing" places at the back of the wagon to the weakest men, or men who were sick. It was easiest to slack off there without attracting attention. We let them push the trailer so they didn't have to push themselves.

+ + +

When we turn into the yard of the Praezifix factory on the third or fourth day, the chief engineer starts yelling at us immediately.

"Where's the furnace man? The bastard has let my central heating go out twice!"

Stani Suske is already taking off his glasses in anticipation of being boxed on the ear. This time he doesn't get hit—he's replaced instead.

"Who can do a better job?"

At first no one comes forward. Then I volunteer.

We have no reason to annoy such a powerful man, and above all we don't want to lose our assignment to the factory.

Then I am taken to see my new domain.

+ + +

It is a little paradise.

Every morning, as soon as we have reported to the factory and been officially signed in, I ring the doorbell at the villa, the chief engineer's private quarters. The door pops open, and I am standing in the hallway.

It is a strange feeling to be a prisoner and find oneself alone in a private house.

"Furnace man!" I shout up to the second floor. Upstairs somewhere I hear a door closing, and no one pays any more attention to me.

I turn right and go straight to the cellar, closing the cellar door carefully behind me. I wedge a little piece of coal under it so I'll hear if someone should start to come down the stairs . . .

Then I'm alone. What that means can be understood only by someone who has grown used to performing even the most private bodily functions under observation . . .

Around me there are four walls, the enormous furnace for the central heating, a pile of coal, a stack of firewood, and a block of wood where it is more comfortable to sit than in the best easy chair at home.

It is wonderfully warm, and my heart leaps for joy.

+ + +

To start with I rap a few times sharply on the furnace with the long iron poker, just to let the people in the house know that something is happening downstairs.

I take care of the furnace in short order. I don't carry the ashes out, though, until I've been in the cellar for a fairly long time and start to worry that if I don't put in an appearance soon the capo or a guard might come to find out what is going on.

Next I choose a few especially fine specimens from the crate of potatoes and bury them in the hot ashes in the grate. I am aware that by so doing I am risking my life. In my imagination I can already hear someone bellowing, "You're all alike, you filthy priests! Hypocrites and thieves! You preach to everyone else, but as for yourselves . . . !" But hunger is a poor counselor.

Several times I go up to the yard on some pretext or other in order to make sure on my return that the house doesn't smell of roast potatoes . . .

And then comes the great moment: In my whole life I have never eaten anything as fine.

+ + +

"What does the bastard do down there the whole day?"

He splits wood for kindling — to matchstick size, actually. And when the crate is full, then he sends the entire contents flying through the furnace door in one go and starts in very carefully again.

He shovels coal . . . from one corner to another and then back to the first corner.

He sweeps and dusts and brushes things off.

In fact, he has taken the whole furnace apart and is

never finished when they need him outside for another task . . .

+ + +

Once the door upstairs creaks.

Like a flash I have the axe in my hand and am splitting wood. But nobody comes. I can't see the door, since the stairs go around a corner.

Then from upstairs I hear a small child's voice: "Mister, are you there?"

I am incapable of describing the impression this voice made on me. A greeting from another world! Did such a thing still exist?

At the same time I felt horribly afraid that someone might find me talking to this child . . .

I still can't see to the top of the stairs and am very careful not to take even one step.

"What are you doing here?" — My tone of voice was intended to be harsh, but I didn't succeed very well.

"You won't tell my mommy, promise?"

"Go back to your mother right now! You'll get dirty down here!"

The little girl went but called back through a crack in the door: "I'll come back tomorrow!"

The next day I was just on my way upstairs with a pail of ashes when I heard a woman's shrill voice calling, "Mathilde, where are you going?"

"To talk to the nice man," the little girl answered.

My heart skipped a beat. What would happen now?

Nothing happened. The girl started down the steps and no one interfered. So the mother didn't mind!

I heaved a sigh of relief.

I never saw the child. On each visit she would push the door open and sit down on the upper steps; then a lively conversation developed between the two of us that was like a ray of light from heaven for me. I told the little girl the most wonderful stories. And thawed in the process myself. I rediscovered my faith in beauty and purity, in innocence and love.

It was all right with me that I never got a glimpse of her. Perhaps she wore long braids, even wore them coiled snail-fashion over her ears, or had some other feature of the master race. As it was I could picture her to myself as the epitome of everything amiable, a messenger from that better world in which I could hardly believe anymore.

And it did me good.

+ + +

"Vive Letzeburg!"

The shout came from a group of prisoners in the convict company, who were shoveling snow along the side of the road.

I had just time to recognize Théophile Becker, the parish priest of Fingig, then we and our vehicle had already passed.

It was the last time I saw him.

+ + +

From the time of my leave I had brought back to Théophile Becker the promise that he would be released soon.

It happened like this: Hartmann, the head of the Gestapo, was a patient at the St. Zitha Clinic then, being looked after by Father Becker's brother. To ensure that the young attendant took good care of him, Hartmann promised to see to it that his brother would be freed before long. An exact date was even specified, and I was supposed to deliver this good news to Father Becker personally. That was no simple matter, since both priests and the members of the convict company were kept isolated from the other camp inmates and had special guards. At last, however, I succeeded in smuggling a scrap of paper to him with the date of his release.

In actual fact Théophile Becker did leave the camp on the date in question with other prisoners. He was put on an "invalid transport" and never seen again . . .

+ + +

One morning we deliver cement to the "New Praezifix."

By the time we unload it we are almost collapsing from exhaustion. With the hundred-pound sacks on our backs we stagger along the narrow planks of the construction scaffolding.

A few minutes before twelve we are finished and drop dead-tired onto the floor of our shed. Someone takes the lid off the soup pail, since the siren ought to signal the midday break at any moment now.

Instead the door suddenly flies open, and an SS man bellows, "So that's what's going on! Just wait, I'll teach you a thing or two!"

With one bound he tips the pail over, so its entire contents flow into the sand.

"On your feet and march! March!"

The monster then stands at the door and hits every man on the head with a board as he goes by.

+ + +

We hitch ourselves up and head out to the factory at a gallop.

So no food, no midday rest!

The guards, who are thus also deprived of both, are furious. As soon as we have gone around the first curve, they order us to stop.

"We're staying right where we are now and eating lunch. Anyone who leaves will be shot!"

What to do? Under no circumstances can someone come across us stopped outside the camp or the factory area at midday.

The capo negotiates with the guards. He knows his fellow capo in charge of the "foxes' den" where the turnips and carrots are stored. He proposes that we take refuge behind it, hide the wagon behind the building and spend our midday break there.

After a lot of back and forth the guards agree. Quickly we load up some rocks and wood that is lying around and set out for the "foxes' den." We run, to make it look as if we are on an urgent mission.

We make it through safely.

+ + +

The "foxes' den" is a magnificent little spot. A kind

of large barn, it lies partly above and partly below ground. There is access to the building only from one side, and any "visitor" can be seen approaching from a long way away.

Inside, however, are mountains of gorgeous turnips, as big as a man's head, and carrots the size of bowling pins. Our eyes widen in amazement.

The guards make themselves comfortable somewhere or other. We camouflage the wagon with straw and twigs. The capo joins his mates around the fire. And we fell on the vegetables like wild animals.

A blow with a spade splits one into three or four pieces, and then we sink our teeth into them. But in a hurry, since it might occur to someone to forbid it! Our bellies hadn't been that full for a long time.

Unfortunately the episode had consequences. The SS man at the "New Praezifix" reported us for "breaking off work early," and our capo was replaced.

During those same weeks Batty Esch suffered a rapid and terrible decline in his strength.

Although the crew of the "marsh express" had shorter distances to run than the "Transport Commando Praezifix," they had more — and heavier — loads to haul between the camp train station, the potato cellar, the foxes' den, and the kitchen. And worst of all: They ate their midday meal in the barrack, so there was never any chance of picking up some extra food.

For that reason I filled myself up with as much turnip soup as my body could stand during the day, to be able to share my bread with Batty in the evenings.

As it turned out, Wampach had been assigned to

cleaning the SS men's barracks, an occasional work detail where the crew also had a chance to come across something edible while sweeping up or emptying the garbage pails. So he did the same thing I was doing and gave some of his "extra" bread to his roommates Stoffels and Brachmond.

Smuggling anything into the camp from an external work detail was as good as impossible, however.

+ + +

Nevertheless I tried it once.

I put two lovely roasted potatoes from the stores of my employer in my pocket and decided simply to take the risk. Esch had headed out to work that morning dizzy from hunger, and I couldn't bear the thought of returning home empty-handed.

But as we came through the gate that evening — late, as we almost always were — I got a terrible jolt: All the work details were lined up there for inspection. They were being "frisked"! First I tried to sneak around the wagon and throw the two potatoes between the wheels without being seen. But we were being too closely observed. I was lost.

The SS platoon leader came toward us and ordered: "Turn out your pockets!"

And then I was rescued: The camp commandant appeared for the evening head count.

"Dismissed!"

We dashed pell-mell between the rows of our mates, who had long since taken up their positions.

+ + +

Batty Esch greeted me with the news that Monsignor Origer was in the camp!

He knew nothing further. Someone had brought him the news.

On the following Sunday we wanted to try to say hello to him at the newcomers' barrack.

When Sunday arrived, however, we both were assigned to punishment detail, because our bed-making had not found favor in the eyes of the room's head prisoner.

For our lapse we were condemned to work in the "gold mine." That meant filling buckets with the contents of the latrine and emptying them on the grass in front of the barrack.

For our buckets the head prisoner chose ones with no handles.

✦ ✦ ✦

In those days a skin cream was available in the canteen with the brand name "Couteline." It had been seized somewhere abroad by the SS, who were making an illegal profit by selling it here. It came in very handy for us, since it was suitable for the many skin problems prevalent in the camp: eczema, scabies, flea bites and the like, abrasions, injuries from beatings or falls, scald wounds, and chilblains.

One evening I saw someone spreading it on his bread.

"There's fat in it," he said.

"Yes, but from animals that died of disease!"

If only I had kept my mouth shut! The man threw up everything he had eaten.

Others were less concerned, until an order came down from the barrack head prisoner: It is forbidden to eat Couteline!

✦ ✦ ✦

Through the efforts of our friend Lorang from Vianden, who had already performed so many useful services for us, Father Wampach found regular work, too. He was assigned to a commando that opened the clamps[1] of turnips and sorted the good ones from the bad ones. The clamps were situated along the road that we passed several times a day with our Praezifix wagon.

Wampach would toss me an especially juicy turnip, and I would reciprocate with a roasted potato from the cellar of the chief engineer at Praezifix.

This provided variety in our menu. But we had to be terribly careful.

✦ ✦ ✦

In the last days of March a report went around that seventeen "policemen" from Luxembourg had been interned at the camp. They were supposed to have refused to take the oath of loyalty to the Führer. We heard that their heads weren't shaved, that special

[1] A clamp is a construction for storing potatoes and other root vegetables over the winter, once frequently used in northern Europe. A hole is dug in the ground and lined with straw; then the vegetables are piled up to above ground level, covered with more straw, and finally with earth. The "clamp" is thus partly below ground and partly above. –Translator's note.

rules applied to them, and when they turned in their clothes a rosary had been found on each of them.

In reality they were members of our former company of volunteer soldiers.

It took a long time until we found an opportunity to say hello to the new arrivals.

After that, however, a friendship arose that will remain a fond memory for the rest of my life. Our soldiers were permitted to write home only once a year. We developed a system of secret arrangements for conveying messages between our newfound friends and their relatives through our own biweekly correspondence. For their part the boys used their access to certain privileges to help us make it through many stretches of hunger.

+ + +

Before the terrible winter of 1942 ended it presented us with tremendous amounts of snow again. So once more the priests had to face the dreaded circus of shoveling and carting or carrying away snow under the blows of the capos and SS. All those assigned to regular work considered themselves fortunate to escape this torment.

True, we had to clear the Praezifix yard and the roads to the factory from ice and snow with pickaxes and shovels, but that was permitted to take place as a humane form of labor somehow, without the supplement of sadism customary within the camp.

+ + +

Our new capo was a nasty fellow. The large amount of running required of the Praezifix commando didn't appeal to him. And since he believed that he had good prospects for assignment to a less strenuous work detail, he pursued only one goal: to wreck our wagon, since it was already in poor condition and he knew that no replacement was available.

He knew, too, that we wouldn't denounce him. After all, we were priests. He turned a deaf ear to all our pleas.

And so loads were piled on the vehicle until its wobbly wheels groaned. We had to run at a gallop through ditches and potholes, until one day the right front wheel shattered. It was a miracle that none of us was injured.

+ + +

The result was not the end of our commando, however, but rather that of Transport Commando 2. The breakdown meant the loss of work and bread for Batty Esch.

His crew's wagon was assigned to us. But because several days had elapsed in the meantime, and because of other difficulties the capo had caused, a discussion started between Praezifix and the camp administration that ended with the factory dispensing with our services.

The capo had achieved his goal.

To be sure, he now tried to keep the work detail together and have it assigned to a new task, but it was the end of our double ration of soup. It also spelled the end of my time sitting in the comfortable cellar and roasting potatoes at the chief engineer's villa.

Easter Week 1942

As we waited to be given a new task we were once again "unassigned": crammed together in the clergy block, suffering hunger, ordered to perform exercises during the day and vulnerable to all kinds of harassment and abuse. There we experienced, as if under a curse, one of the worst weeks in all my time in the camp.

It was Easter Week of 1942.

On Good Friday we had spent the whole morning in the pouring rain in the assembly yard. From there we marched to the kitchen to pick up and carry the food pails.

Afterwards, as we neared our barrack, number 30 — dead tired, soaked, and famished — we were confronted with a sight that took our breath away.

The entire contents of our room — tables, stools, straw mattresses, and the contents of all the lockers, meaning bread, towels, bowls, spoons, etc. — lay strewn in complete disorder on the rain-sodden barrack street. The windows and doors were open.

"Fall in!"

"One of you bastards was hiding foreign currency, and it was found! As a punishment everything in blocks 28 and 30 will be thrown outside twice a day for the next week. Twice a day you will put it back in perfect order, everything cleaned off, and the beds re-made. You will dust and sweep until not one piece of straw is visible on the street. There will be no food until evening, and then only after the clerk has made a personal inspection."

We stood rooted to the spot in horror.

All of us realized immediately that the pretext was just that: a pretext. In view of the treatment to which entering prisoners were subjected, how would it have been possible to smuggle even the smallest amount of foreign money into the camp? And what would have been the point of it in the first place?

Someone claimed to know that there was a reason behind it: The Vatican radio station had broadcast a critical report about Dachau and protested the mistreatment of priests.

+ + +

I don't know if the reader can imagine what it means when something like 750 sacks filled with straw, most of them torn, the same number of wedge-shaped pillows,

and 500 blankets are lying helter-skelter in mud and
rain — not to mention furniture and all one's personal
belongings. Or what it means when all of this is
supposed to be put back in place during the one-hour
midday break: the beds made, the rooms swept and
dusted, and not even the tiniest speck of straw
remaining in the barrack street . . .

+ + +

When the signal growled, we had actually done it
and restored order.

Then we had to exercise for the entire afternoon.
Meaning the form of exercise used for punishment,
with running, "up and down" exercises, and deep knee
bends.

On our return we met with the same chaos as in the
morning. And a new round of the dance began.

Only when everything was finished and sparkling
clean were we allowed to eat; after that we dropped
half-dead onto the beds that we had made, to an insane standard of precision, just moments earlier.

+ + +

So it went, day after day.

Twice a day, while we completed our punishment
exercise routine, the personnel of the working barracks
came and emptied out our rooms, tossing everything in
them onto the streets and stealing whatever they could
lay their hands on in the process.

And the same number of times we put everything
back, and were allowed to eat only mornings and evenings.

The balance at the end of the week: Between 70 and 80 dead and a steep decline in the strength and vitality of the 1,500 hundred inmates in the two clergy barracks that were affected.

It was like a deliverance when on the fifth day — it was the Tuesday after Easter — our capo turned up and led the seventeen men of the former Praezifix commando off to work.

We were assigned a meadow in the vicinity of the "foxes' den," which we were to dig up and turn into a field ready for sowing in the shortest possible time.

The work showed us how pitifully weak we had become. There was no extra ration, because we weren't performing "serious" labor. The only one to get his bread was the capo, who stood around watching us.

+ + +

Since all the other members of the crew were Polish, the capo sometimes started a conversation with me during work, and I seized the opportunity to catch my breath without risking punishment. In these talks we spoke only about religion and religious matters. Sometimes the guards chimed in, too. At the end of them my adversaries always had the last word: "It's all nonsense and lies! And now get back to work!"

Once I had a guard who had obviously received some education, and I managed to get the better of him completely. I explained to him how, if God has created man with free will, He has to leave a back door open for unbelief despite all His revelations of Himself. For if He showed Himself to us too clearly, He would force us to believe and thus, having given us freedom with one hand, take it away with the other.

Another time I did something most unwise. After we had spoken for a whole morning about religious matters, the capo said, "I'm not changing my mind — I still don't believe in God!" Unable to resist the temptation, I responded, "Why do you talk about Him so much then?"

That put an abrupt end to our theological conversations.

+ + +

We were happiest when a transport of turnips — or even better, carrots — passed the field where we were working on its route from the "foxes' den" to the kitchen. Then a few of the juicy things would happen to roll off the wagon, as if by accident, and if the guards weren't really nasty fellows we could satisfy the worst pangs of hunger for a while.

+ + +

"The mayor of Vienna is here," Esch said one day when I got home. "His name is Schmitz. I know him well from various congresses. He's going to try to get me a good assignment."

Schmitz had been in the camp for a long time and had acquired some useful connections.

A few days later Esch and Father Brachmond were assigned to the crew in the "dry storage room" at the plantation, where the Polish bishop Monsignor Cozal was working.

It was light work under a roof, and even if the crudely built storeroom was cold and drafty, the work crew there got the extra bread ration. Their task was to sort the plants grown and dried at the plantation, various cooking and medicinal herbs, and pack them in small bags for shipping.

Hunger

We hadn't dug up even a third of our meadow when suddenly a new order was given: All priests were to work at the plantation, but without the extra ration. This was on the 19th of April.

Our commando was disbanded, and on the following morning the 1,500 non-German priests marched directly from the assembly yard through the south gate.

It goes without saying that we were not assigned to the actual plantation itself, which was like a large commercial nursery with all kinds of interesting plants, and where there were tolerable work details. No, we were sent to an area planned for expansion, a square tract measuring about a quarter of a mile on a side, which was to be prepared with paths, ditches, and dikes, and thereby transformed from a patch of the Dachau marshes into agricultural land.

It was heavy labor under the feared regimen of a notorious capo named Rasch.

For most of the priests this meant the beginning of the end.

Immediately after we arrived at the new field to be created for the plantation we were divided into groups of 30 men, each under its own capo. Some groups were given wheelbarrows, the others shovels and spades.

As its first task my commando is supposed to carry gravel to the furthest end of a path that is being extended, where 12 men are pushing a roller. The wheelbarrows are heavy, and on the rough uneven gravel a number of ours break on the very first morning.

A little before nine o'clock two prisoners approach our work area carrying a big basket. Are we going to get the extra bread ration after all? Wild hopes spring up in us.

They actually come right up to us.

"Priests?"

"Yes."

They laugh scornfully and keep going. Only the capo gets a nice big piece of bread with sausage.

+ + +

The time drags terribly from half-past six to noon. On every round with the wheelbarrow I think it must be the last.

Suddenly I notice how much the hideous week of harassment, the extra exercises for punishment and the lack of food have weakened me.

When at long last the flag is waved at the far end of

the field, as a sign that work is over, I almost faint from hunger and fatigue.

Nonetheless we are ordered to run there at a trot, where the "better class" of plantation prisoners have already fallen in to march back to camp. They greet us with curses because we made them wait . . .

+ + +

As we are marching back I run into Batty Esch.

"Monsignor Origer has been moved to the invalid barrack. Schmitz told me."

We didn't know whether to be happy or not, since rumors were already circulating that the inmates of this block were taken away in groups and dispatched in some way.

In the invalid barrack Monsignor Origer encountered Father Stoffels, who had been declared "unfit for work" and sent there after a long stay in the infirmary.

+ + +

The time allotted for eating is extremely short.

First the 100 occupants of each room must take turns washing their shoes until they are spotless in the five available basins, stow them in their lockers, take their places at the table and wait as quiet as mice. Only then is the lid of the soup pail removed.

As soon as we've bolted down the soup we wash the bowls, tidy up and sweep the room, and then it's already time for the midday head count.

+ + +

In the afternoon there is easier work to do.

We carry loam in tin buckets to a square of the field to enrich the marshy soil. Like figures on carousel we march in a circle in single file, filling the buckets from a truck and emptying them on the field as we walk.

As long as Rasch, the capo, is not visible we are not harried. There just has to be constant movement. When you reach the truck with your empty bucket it's even possible, now and then, to walk by without filling it and start the circle again . . .

Our work area lies at the edge of the field. There is no demarcation of the boundary, which can be imagined only by drawing an invisible line connecting the guards' platforms.

One of us steps aside to relieve himself.

A shot rings out.

Had the man crossed the boundary? Was it only a warning? In any event he wasn't hit and races back to us white as a sheet, where he is beaten almost to a pulp by the capo.

+ + +

There are fresh arrivals from Luxembourg in block 9!

The very same day we have a chance to greet Father Dupong and Professor Emil Schaus, at least through the barbed wire.

It is always a strange feeling to know that a good friend is in the newcomers' block, one that alternates between regret and happiness. The happiness comes from seeing a dear face again and knowing that person is near, and to hear news from home.

I can't recall what news the "novices" brought us. All I remember is what an enormous consolation their arrival meant for Esch and me.

+ + +

"You can eat this," a Czech priest instructs me as we move along a row on our knees, pulling up weeds.

He holds up a black something, about the length of a finger.

"It is the root of a plant that contains fat. I don't know what it's called. I just know where it grows, and I want to show it to you. A friend of mine ate some. It's very nourishing . . ."

Later we pass a clump of it with our wheelbarrow. It happens to be the only place where we can set the barrow down more or less unseen. My friend pulls on a leafy stem and hauls up a root with several branches.

I scrape it off with a sharp-edged stone and quickly put it in my mouth. The thing is greasy and doesn't really taste of anything at all, but it leaves a nasty slippery coating on my tongue.

Later I felt a little sick to my stomach, and I never touched the plant again.

+ + +

There are other things you can eat.

First and foremost there are dandelions. You simply pull one up, roots and all, shake the dirt off, and stick the whole thing in your mouth. Unfortunately there aren't many of them where we are working. To find them you have to search along the edges of the muddy ditches, but furtively, without making yourself conspicuous.

Much better tasting are the newly planted peas and beans, which have just poked a shoot through the soil and been softened by the moisture. But one has to be especially careful, since first of all it is theft and secondly sabotage!

In one corner of our area there must have been some rhubarb growing the year before, for here and there a pink stem is sticking out of the ground. If you come across something like that, you have to note the exact spot and then often spend days seeking a pretext to bend down in that particular place, as if by chance. That's if someone else hasn't discovered the juicy morsel in the meantime . . .

What makes us happiest of all is being assigned some task that takes us near the compost heap.

With a little luck you can find a lot of things that are still quite edible, such as the outer leaves of red cabbages or leek and chive seedlings that have been thrown away after thinning . . .

+ + +

For a few days now I have been eyeing a dandelion on a fat stem at the edge of the road we take to march home.

I'm not the only one casting longing glances at the fine specimen. Many pairs of eyes scan the road ahead when our column approaches the spot, observe with satisfaction that the dandelion is still there, hesitate, and . . . once again the opportunity has been lost.

I have sworn that the plant will be mine. One day when the capo is on the other side of the column and I myself am at the far right end of a row, I throw my cap on the flower in a split second as we go past, dash out of formation and retrieve my cap. I pull up the plant with it and put them both on my head.

+ + +

"I've stolen something," Batty Esch says with a sly smile as we retire to our corner of the bunk room carrying our full soup bowls.

He takes my hand and puts it in his pocket. I feel a pulverized substance, a fine dust.

"That is soup powder. It's a mixture of different vegetables that have been dried and finely ground. There a whole sack full of it at the plantation storage room. I bet it will be good in our soup. The bishop took some, too."

If his last remark was intended to banish any moral scruples I might have had, it was superfluous. Each of us dropped a large handful into our carrot soup.

But guess what happened next! The stuff began to rise like cake batter, the whole soup turned thick and stiff and took on such a fiery hot taste that after the first spoonful we had to rush out to cool our burning mouths at the water faucet.

The soup was inedible.

+ + +

The worst was still to come.

When we came in from the field at noon on the

following day, there was considerable excitement in front of the plantation greenhouse. Two miserable figures were kneeling on the pavement, their faces turned to the wall. When we marched back to the camp they remained behind with a guard. It was raining and a cold wind was blowing.

"They are two priests who stole something," says a capo triumphantly. "If they haven't snuffed it by tonight, they'll get 25 lashes on their bare backs. They're all alike!"

A terrible suspicion crossed my mind, which unfortunately was soon confirmed.

Batty Esch and Brachmond were missing at the midday meal . . .

As we marched past the greenhouse in the afternoon, the unhappy souls were still kneeling there, but completely naked, and SS louts were pouring buckets of water over them from the upper story.

While we were working someone was able to tell us what had happened.

Their work crew had been unexpectedly frisked, and bits of green dust, traces of their "theft" on the previous morning, had been found in Brachmond and Esch's pockets. It was not until the evening head count that they returned to the camp, more dead than alive.

"It's going to be reported," said Esch, "and we'll both be kicked off the drying room work crew. But the worst of it is that we've let Schmitz down. I have to go see him right away tomorrow."

The mayor of Vienna had indeed used all of his influence to get the two priests assigned to such a fine commando, and now they had turned out to be thieves!

Another thought was also unbearable for Batty Esch.

"My poor mother," he must have said twenty times on that evening. "In the drying room crew maybe I could have made it through. Now it's all over. And it's my own fault. It serves me right. But my poor mother . . ."

"It's not so bad in our commando," I said, trying to console him. "Now and then you find something to eat. And when everything starts to grow, the carrots and the turnips . . . Yesterday somebody from the greenhouse commando gave me a small head of red cabbage . . ."

But as I spoke I suddenly felt faint and had to lie down quickly on the straw mattress. Batty noticed.

"We'll go together soon . . .," he said, as he lay down beside me.

"Yes," I said, and then we fell asleep.

The next day the two "thieves" were assigned to our commando, with the comment that they "were being punished."

The actual report was never filed, however, and so they escaped the punishment of 25 lashes with a horse-whip or "2 hours on the tree," i.e. being hung by their arms, that would have inevitably followed.

It came about like this: A short time before Brachmond had let the SS officer who managed the plantation know that he was a bee-keeper. Now bees were the officer's hobby, and he had a beautiful apiary in the old wall of the plantation. So Brachmond was brought in to see the severe taskmaster to take an exam and, if he passed it, be assigned to the beekeeping work crew.

The manager at once recognized Brachmond as one of the thieves who had been caught a few days earlier.

And so, first of all, the unfortunate prisoner was given a good thrashing and castigated: "How could he ever have dared?" . . . etc.

But then a kind of psychological and diplomatic duel ensued: The officer kept on shouting about thievery and depraved priests, while Brachmond spoke only of honey and sweet things.

And he won.

Brachmond didn't get assigned to the bee commando, nor were he and Esch returned to the dry storage room, but they escaped being reported.

+ + +

We had terrible weather during those weeks. It rained almost constantly, and an icy wind drove the clouds over the unprotected plain.

We had not had overcoats for a long time, and so we were often soaked to the skin when we arrived at our work area.

If we were digging ditches and making dikes, we could sometimes crouch down so that from a distance it looked as if we were digging with our hands, when in reality we were trying to protect ourselves behind the one-and-a-half-foot-high dike from the awful wind and rain for a few minutes.

Once Rasch, the capo, caught someone who had turned up the collar of his jacket.

He gave an order for everyone in the entire field: "Jackets off!" So hundreds of us had to work for the rest of the morning in our shirt sleeves.

+ + +

As long as we were working in the same commando, Esch and I spent the half hour between coffee and head count every morning in reflection together.

While the prisoners on clean-up duty swept and dusted, all the inmates in our room had to go out to the barrack street anyway. We would then walk up and down, exchanging thoughts and trying to keep each other's spirits up. If one can no longer pray alone, then it is still possible in company. Afterwards we confessed and gave one another absolution.

It was a great comfort for us. We felt calmer and more serene, and that did us good physically.

Occasionally Emile Schaus would join us.

In early May we learned that Théophile Becker had been sent "on a transport."

I couldn't believe it at first. Hadn't Hermann, the head of the Gestapo, assured me that Becker would be released soon?

When we heard the news, we prayed the *De Profundis* as we worked.

+ + +

Wampach and I are supposed to plant willow saplings along a path.

I was so dizzy that I often had to remeasure the intervals several times. We both had only one thought: to reach the hedge, where we would be able to rest for a moment unobserved and take shelter from the wind and rain.

Behind the hedge Wampach pulled out a cigarette end and a match.

"It'll give you a boost, you'll see."

I had given up smoking months before. First of all to stay stronger and better able to hold out, but also because with the few cigarettes we came by here and there one could recruit advantageous friends.

I took a puff, then a second — and suddenly without any warning I was seized by the collar and thrown to the ground, while punches and kicks rained down on me.

It was Rasch, the capo! I barely had time to recognize him when he was gone again.

Yet suddenly I found my inner balance again. It was as if the blows had shaken me out a dangerous state of self-abandonment and resignation, and reawakened my will to live.

The western edge of our work area is occupied by several rows of magnificent rhubarb plants.

How often we cast longing glances in that direction, and if our task takes us only in the vicinity of the juicy stalks our hearts beat faster. But the guards are too near, and since the rhubarb marks the line past which they are to shoot any prisoner, they keep an extremely sharp eye on it.

"The rhubarb is blossoming!" Batty Esch had exclaimed a few days earlier. And now enormous flowers are waving at the top of stems several feet tall.

As luck would have it, a visit to the plantation is scheduled for tomorrow. The SS manager discovers the problem of the blossoms as he is making a final inspection of the area to make sure that everything is ready for the visitors. He curses and fumes and threatens to remove all the capos if all the blossoms are not cut off within the next two hours — and cut so carefully that the visitors won't notice anything.

We are given knives and baskets and fall to work right away. We don't feel particularly comfortable, though, since the machine guns are immediately trained on us from the different watchtowers.

None of us dares to cut off even one of the juicy leaves.

"Well then, we'll just eat the flower stems," I say to Esch and Wampach, who are sharing a basket with me.

"No," says Esch. "They're no good. Don't know why, but the flower stalks are always thrown away."

I dismiss this as ignorance, and when we carry the full basket to the compost heap, I cut off a clean piece of stalk and find that what is supposedly "no good" tastes excellent. Now the others hold back no longer.

When we head toward the compost heap with the second basketful, all three of us are having trouble walking in a straight line . . . We feel "so unusual, so light and yet pe-cu-li-ar."[1] We stagger as if we were carrying God only knows how heavy a load. On reaching the compost we fall on top of the heap with the basket, laughing uproariously, and can barely get back on our feet.

What drug lurks in the flower stalks of the rhubarb plant will have to be determined by botanists. The

[1] In the original: *"Uns ist so wunderlich, so leicht und doch absunderlich."* This is a quotation from *Hans Huckebein,* a tale in verse about a pet raven that samples too much liqueur and meets a bad end, by the popular 19th-century German humorist Wilhelm Busch. –Translator's note.

greater puzzle to my mind is why no one noticed what condition we were in.

But they say that drunks have a special guardian angel.

Visitors in the Camp

When we returned for the midday meal, we were not allowed into the camp, but had to wait outside the gate for ages.

At first we thought that they might be frisking everybody, and the entire column was seized with great anxiety. If someone didn't have a cigarette end on him, then he had brought along a few dandelion leaves or some other edible weed for his soup.

Then we learned the reason for the delay: visitors to the camp! That meant in effect: no meal and no midday break, but instead hours of standing and waiting, for the visitors must find the camp empty without fail. The external work crews have to stay outside, and all the prisoners in the camp must vanish into the barracks as quickly as possible and remain there, as still as mice, with the windows and doors closed.

Only a few well-nourished capos are supposed to be visible, walking casually up and down the camp street between the lawn and the decorative saplings, and looking contented. In the assembly yard the camp band is concertizing in competition with the first twittering birds of spring.

Visitors always follow the same route: They are shown the changing room and the showers, view their own reflections in the tiles on the kitchen floor and the giant cooking vat polished to a high gloss, and nod approvingly at the laundry, disinfection site and clothes storage. Then it's on to the infirmary, which is equipped with the last word in modern medical technology. And finally they visit a barrack. The nearest one, of course, and that is barrack 2 — as if by sheer chance. There room 4 has been turned into a real showplace. The floor is waxed, the beds made up with spotless linen; everything exudes tranquility and comfort. At one table sit a half dozen "honor inmates" without shaved heads, whose job it is to manage this jewel, keeping it ready to be inspected at all times. "Unfortunately the other inmates happen to be outside working at the moment . . ."

In reality they are standing outside the gate, shivering from hunger and fatigue, following the visitors through the camp in their imaginations and wondering anxiously if there will be enough time left to eat their midday soup.

On that day several of our fellows simply collapsed. We delivered them to the infirmary afterwards and never saw them again.

This does not necessarily mean that they were murdered. But prisoners were so afraid of the infirmary — or at the very least of the procedure for getting admitted to it — that everyone who didn't have some special contact there did his utmost to stay on his feet as long as possible. If he broke down despite it, then his strength had usually declined to the point where recovery was no longer possible.

+ + +

Finally we were allowed to march inside.

But no sooner had we gone through the gate than the camp runner came dashing over from the officer of the day, yelling at the capos, "Are you crazy? The visitors are still here! Get out of sight immediately!"

We scattered like startled wild animals and made a run for it without instructions, taking cover behind the far ends of the barracks.

When the danger was finally past, we were granted an extra half hour — we could hardly believe our ears — so that there would be time to eat.

+ + +

"All priests report to the kitchen!" Since the foreign priests had started working in the plantation the German clergy, who had no other work assignment, had to carry the food pails to all the barracks. Today all of us had to pitch in so that it would go faster.

We are so weakened, however, that countless numbers of us can no longer lift the heavy containers. The stronger ones have to make two or three trips. By the time we are done the time is up. The signal growls for the end of the midday break, and we march off to work without having eaten.

At the End of Our Strength

The following Sunday is Pentecost, one of the first warm days that year.

It was already clear to us that some form of harassment is planned for the clergy block, as on all Church festivals. We don't have to wait long to find out what it is.

"Thirty men report from each room!"

It's my bad luck to be in our group.

We march to the open space in front of the disinfection building, where an enormous heap of scraps of clothing is lying. We recognize the uniforms of the Russian officers who were taken away from the camp some time before; they have been cut into narrow strips.

"Sort the strips by color! There will be nothing to eat until you're finished!"

We fall to it.

"They're still warm . . . ," says someone next to me. Of course the reason is that the strips had just come out of the disinfection equipment. Still, when we reached into the center of the nice warm heap, we couldn't help imagining that we were feeling the body warmth of the murdered men.

My neighbor suddenly bent his head down and vomited into the middle of the pile.

Soon we were feeling so weak and nauseated that we could hardly distinguish the yellow strips from the yellowish-green ones.

When the signal sounded for the evening head count we were nowhere near finished. In fact the scraps were lying in countless large and small heaps scattered all around.

The next day a transport commando with shovels and rakes pushed everything back together and loaded it all onto wagons, which drove away with it.

When it came time to write letters again — soon after Pentecost — I tried to prepare my family for the worst. I had grown so weak that it could be only a matter of days until I collapsed.

Nevertheless I noticed that Batty Esch was suffering more from hunger than I was. On Pentecost Monday I believed that his end was near.

I dashed through the camp as if hounds were after me, from one prisoner to the next. The thought that I wasn't begging for myself but for my friend made me strong. I went to Noppeney, to Jis Thorn, to Lorang. I went to see our young soldiers. It was not in vain.

Esch wept when I unpacked. But then the mood of despair seized him again that had become increasingly prevalent in him recently. "What's the use? Now I'm eating all the others' food, too, and it's still just a drop in the ocean."

+ + +

On May 28 (if I remember correctly) Father Stoffels turned up unexpectedly at our block, escorted by the infirmary capo.

"I've been assigned to a transport," he said while Father Wampach gathered his few possessions from room 4. When he saw our sad faces he added, "We're simply going to another camp . . . It's supposed to be much better there."

The dear, good man! He just couldn't fathom how far human malice — or rather diabolical wickedness — could go. For a brief moment he remained alone with Father Wampach, and I am sure that Wampach gave him final absolution in parting.

Then he gave all of us a farewell kiss: Wampach, Brachmond, Esch and me.

"Forward march!"

For certain our friend is better off in the "other camp" . . .

+ + +

"The priests are going to be assigned to the crematorium commando," says the head prisoner of our barrack to the clerk. He glances gleefully in our direction and speaks loud enough for us to hear him.

The effect was not at all what the head prisoner had expected, however.

"Then from now on the dead will be buried in the presence of a priest," one of us observes. Someone else has heard that the "material" delivered to the crematorium now and then included people who were still alive, to whom one could give absolution. "At the very least we can secretly say the prayers for the dead."

Unfortunately a few had voiced such thoughts too loudly. The head prisoner made a report and the crematorium commando was not given to us.

The plantation remained our lot, the same as ever.

The most attractive place on the whole plantation was without doubt the latrine, for which the camp language generally used a less formal term.

Originally just a horizontal pole, mounted at a height of about eighteen inches on two posts driven into the ground, on which there was room for four men, the installation was later surrounded by a "curtain" made of old sacks. The reason was less a sense of shame than the need for a few minutes when one could get away from the constant observation of the capos and guards.

Thus it became the classic rendezvous, where one could meet people from all barracks. It was here we fled when we were too tired to keep going. Ten minutes to reach it, ten minutes there (including waiting time), and ten minutes to return made for a half-hour break.

For a while there was even a special latrine capo, whose job was to keep it functioning in an orderly manner.

+ + +

There was still another reason why we liked going to the place.

Right next to it was a huge compost heap, where sometimes we could find something edible.

One day, while Esch and I were waiting in line, a garbage pail of boiled bones was emptied there. At once we threw ourselves on them. The thought indeed occurred to me that the bones probably came from the dog kennels . . . but what difference did that make? Just because an SS dog found nothing more to gnaw on, that didn't mean a prisoner would give up yet.

Another time a capo brought a hand basket full of discarded leek seedlings to the compost. When he saw our longing glances, he tossed them out, then spread his legs and urinated on the pile of them.

"That's so you'll lose your appetites," he said.

He was mistaken, however. I learned on this occasion that some of my fellows were even hungrier than I was . . .

+ + +

"That's number five today," remarks Batty Esch.

I look around cautiously without stopping work. It's Stani Suske, the likable Pole from Posen. Somebody shouts: "Man down!"

One command, and Stani is dragged out of the muddy puddle in which he is lying face down. Left next to the wheelbarrows and the other equipment until work is over.

"Too bad about the fellow," someone says. That he won't recover in the infirmary, where he will now probably end up — everybody knows that.

+ + +

We go on "working." That means pulling out tiny, half-inch high weeds from an endlessly long dike made of dirt we had thrown up.

Is there really no possibility at all of getting into the barrack for the sick before one's health has broken down so completely that it's too late?

"What if I let myself fall on purpose?"

"You're delirious," is Nick Wampach's only response.

+ + +

I needed days to reflect and arrive at a clear conscience. My thoughts moved slowly, as heavy as lead.

"You can try it," the others had finally said.

My rapidly increasing weakness helped my sluggish powers of decision. I had been there the longest and probably had the least to lose. If the attempt was successful, then my friends could follow me.

+ + +

"Now!" I said to Batty, who was jogging next to me.

It was as we were headed back to camp. At a jog, since we were late. Being behind schedule was an advantage, since that meant the procedure for dealing with me would be shortened.

I hit the asphalt hard. And was pleased about it, for I had acted my part well. The column of dead-tired men tumbled on top of me. I hear curses. I'm rolled over with the aid of kicks. Then an order. I'm loaded onto a wheelbarrow, and Batty Esch of all people has to trundle me home.

"On the double, forward march!"

My head is hanging backward over the edge of the barrow and bumping against the wheel. I manage to endure it as piece after piece of my scalp is torn off.

At the assembly yard I am unloaded. The head count takes almost an hour. And it feels so good to be able to lie there while the others are standing at attention. Then the moment of truth arrives. The SS doctor inspects the long row of men reported sick. Most of them by far are returned to duty with punches and kicks. Now my task is to play my part to the end. I hardly need to simulate. I pray to my guardian angel.

The doctor examines me, using his boot as a "stethoscope," then I hear the blessed word "Infirmary!"

It sounded like angels' voices.

The Infirmary

"Number? — Name? — Date of birth?"

I have to turn in the usual prisoner's uniform and receive a fresh shirt and a wool blanket.

"Go lie down!"

I look around. The room is packed, and all the straw sacks, more than a hundred of them, are occupied. In many cases three men on two mattresses. I meet half fearful, half hostile glances from people who are obviously afraid they will have to give up some of their space.

Then someone pulls at my shirt.

"Come lie here next to me."

By now I understand that much Polish. And the look the man gives me says as much as: "I'll be making room for you soon." He is a priest, a professor at a Polish seminary.

+ + +

I can't remember ever feeling so comfortable in my entire life.

To be able to lie quietly! Simply stretch out! Close my eyes and think of nothing! No work, no head count! Nobody will pay any attention to me, and at midday the soup will arrive automatically . . . I recall wondering if it could be any better in heaven.

+ + +

Mealtime! The pails rattle as they come through the door. All heads are raised.

"Barley," I report to my hospitable neighbor, who can no longer sit up. "Oh!" is all he says, in delight.

"Do we get the same ration as outside?" I ask.

My neighbor doesn't answer. He is dead.

Cautiously I turn his head toward me and swiftly and secretly perform my priestly office. In the few hours we had spent together, I had made the acquaintance of a saint.

Quickly I turn him around so that no one will notice my bed-mate is no longer alive; then I get my food, and his, and eat both.

Only then do I call out: "Man dead!"

+ + +

One of the prisoners on room duty, called "attendants" in the infirmary, glances at him briefly, pulls his mouth wide open, and calls over to the clerk: "Two!"

Later I learn that this refers to the number of gold teeth.

Then the dead man's shirt is removed and he is

dragged naked across the floor to the washroom. There he is covered with a blanket (still done at that time!) and left until the next morning, when a cart will take him and the other dead of the previous day to the crematorium.

Now I have a straw sack all to myself.

+ + +

If someone has to get up, he wraps himself in his blanket and totters barefoot to the toilet and washroom.

I have difficulty standing up. It makes me realize just how weak I have grown.

As I walk by the bunks I look at the patients' charts hanging at the end of each bed. They list the name, number, and barrack, then the diagnosis (invariably "general debility" in this room), and below that — I can't believe my eyes — records of temperature and pulse readings! It looks as if we were actually receiving treatment.

"You have to go up to a top bunk," says an attendant when I come back. "You can still climb pretty well. When you can't manage anymore, you'll get a middle bunk, and then one at the bottom."

The explanation was well meant, but it didn't sound very comforting . . . And in fact someone was moved from the top of a bunk down to the middle for me and another man from the middle to the bottom tier. I climbed up, using every last ounce of strength, and took possession of my new mattress, next to a very disagreeable fellow.

+ + +

My neighbor did not respond to my greeting.

But when he makes a motion under the blanket, a wave of nauseating stench reaches my nostrils. At the same time I notice that his sheet — for such things still existed in the infirmary — is caked with blood and pus.

The calves of both his legs are covered with phlegmons.

"Those are edemas filled with pus," a Czech doctor in a nearby bed explains to me later. "In some people hunger leads to water retention and the ordinary swellings we call edema. Death occurs when the water reaches the heart. In others the edemas become gangrenous and are called phlegmons. People with those just slowly rot away."

✦ ✦ ✦

In the evening I help to "bandage" my neighbor.

"I got my last dressing day before yesterday," he says, "but now there's no more linen left."

Then he hands me a roll of toilet paper, which is available from the canteen, and I use it to wrap a good thick layer around both his legs.

I have to summon all my energy to keep from fainting.

I had been in the infirmary for just two days when Batty Esch arrived.

"It didn't go quite as smoothly as with you," he said when I shook his hand. "I got a bad beating first. Brachmond is coming tomorrow, and then Wampach."

"There's no free mattress," I told him. "You'll have to share."

He looked so bad that he was given a place in the middle tier right away.

The two others arrived according to schedule. Brachmond joined us in room 1. Father Wampach was assigned to room 3.

+ + +

"Dressings!"

The call came every Tuesday and Friday. One of the men on room duty laid his broom aside, readied a few knives, scissors and so forth on a table, and pulled out a roll of paper for dressings and a pot of salve.

Then the procedure started.

Whoever had open sores — that included most of us — got in line. Naked, of course, even if the sore was on a finger or a foot.

Sores never heal in Dachau. Is the vitamin-poor diet the cause, or the general debility and the resulting accumulation of water almost everywhere under the skin?

When it's the turn of the people with phlegmons, strong nerves are required. For instance an attendant, unflinchingly and with amazing dexterity, plunges a knife finger-deep into a badly swollen calf, and then repeats the process from the other side with another knife so that the two blades meet. Blood, pus, and water just pour out. After that a very long and thick needle is pushed through the whole calf with the blunt end and eye first; a cloth soaked in a fluid is threaded into the eye and then pulled back through the wound by the pointed end of the needle. The rag is left in the wound so that it doesn't close. Everyone who can manage to stand upright flees outside to escape the appalling stench.

+ + +

That evening my neighbor kept ripping his dressings off.

The smell had grown simply beyond endurance. In addition it was hot under the ceiling in the top tiers of the bunks. But what use was it that all the men around us were cursing and making threats?

During the night I had the feeling that someone was meddling with my bed-mate. I took my bread and stashed it under the blanket. Then I fell asleep again.

In the morning my neighbor was dead.

A terrible suspicion dawned on me. A glance from the man in the bunk opposite confirmed it: The look in his eyes was that of a madman. He had strangled my bed-mate.

Was it because he couldn't stand the hideous smell anymore? Or was his objective my neighbor's bread? In any case that had disappeared.

I said nothing. What good would it have done? Probably it would just have directed suspicion toward me.

And — shall I admit it? Secretly I was glad to be rid of such an awful neighbor.

+ + +

"Everyone out of bed! Fall in!"

At once wild rumors abounded. "We're going to be

gassed!" exclaimed some. "No," said others, "they're making room, and those of us in decent shape will have to go back to work."

We have to fall in outside and parade, each miserable figure holding his chart, in front of an SS man whose indescribably vicious expression I will remember for a long time.

It is precisely this expression on his face that gave me a premonition: In this instance pretending to be healthy would be the wiser tactic. So I summoned every ounce of strength at my disposal and marched as straight as an arrow past the powerful figure.

A few days later about twenty of the most pitiable men were led away. I don't know what happened to them.

+ + +

None of my friends was among them.

After a week in the infirmary Brachmond developed phlegmons everywhere. Within a few days his whole body was covered with them. When he returned from bandaging, he was wrapped in paper from head to foot so that he looked like a mummy.

The head attendant began calling him "the ghost."

Everywhere I went I had always told stories of Brachmond's heroic deeds in the Resistance, and word of them had reached even the head attendant's ears. That gained Brachmond a certain amount of good will among all the infirmary personnel, and they liked to hear him talk about home.

The phlegmons on his head and neck gave "the

ghost" bad headaches. Then he would see and hear nothing, and pulling out a roll of toilet paper, would draw for hours. Over and over he sketched new models for wooden bee hives . . .

+ + +

As I returned to my bunk from the toilet one morning, I found an excited crowd around it.

"Someone has been caught stealing bread!"

A stab of fear goes through me. I feel around under my straw sack. My bread, nearly half a ration, was gone!

One of the men on room duty shoves a piece of crumpled newspaper in my face: "Is this yours?"

I recognize it at once. There was an article on it about the psychology of children. I must have read it about twenty times since I had started using it every day to wrap up my bread.

"Yes," I say, in the hope of getting my bread back.

I never saw the bread again. But I had uttered a death sentence for someone.

"As he was making his bed, he put his pillow down on the other man's bunk, apparently casually, but when he went to pick it up he reached under the mattress and pulled the bread out with the pillow. When he saw he'd been caught he put it in his mouth and swallowed it!" the man on duty reported to the attendant, who had just arrived.

The guilty man threw me a look. A look of terrible fear, which I will never be able to forget. He was a Pole. "*Miserere me. Sacerdos sum . . .* ," he whispered to me.

I tried to put in a word for the man with the attendant, but before I could finish he punched me in the face.

The unfortunate man was dragged into the washroom and "finished off" . : .

+ + +

I notice that the accumulations of water I have long had in my feet are gradually spreading up my legs, and edemas appear on my face and hands. Wherever I press a finger against my skin, it takes several minutes for the indentation to go away.

I realize that my hour is nearing now.

One morning the attendant pokes his fist into my body and says, "You're a bag of water."

A red *W* is written on my chart, and from then on I get only half a spoonful of soup.

I am also moved from the top tier to the middle one.

+ + +

Since arriving in the infirmary Batty Esch had suffered from a form of diarrhea resembling dysentery.

It was paramount to conceal it, for men with this ailment were labeled with an unvarnished term and moved immediately to room 4, where no one paid any more attention to their condition. If someone could no longer stand up, he just remained lying in his excrement until death released him.

One day after we had been in the infirmary for about three weeks, Esch's bunk-mate reported him to the man on room duty. He was expelled to room 4 followed by a chorus of the nastiest obscenities imaginable.

+ + +

Now I saw my friend only occasionally, when we were allowed out into the warm sunshine.

Then we would wrap our blankets around our hips, totter out to the yard using the wall for support and sit down together on the curb of the sidewalk.

Batty was in a terrible state of mind in those days.

Again and again he would bring up the topic of his "theft" and utter the most incredible reproaches against himself.

"I am guilty of my own death. If I had been able to control myself, I could have stayed in the good work crew at the drying room, and maybe I would have made it through . . ."

Or he would repeat: "My poor mother."

Nothing helped, no words of encouragement, no arguments. Often we just sat silently together, I suppose. I would hold his hand in mine, and that did us both good.

One day my guardian angel put the right words in my mouth:

"You stole for my sake," I said. "You shared the green stuff with all of us, didn't you?"

Then he grew calmer. Or at least he pretended to.

Brachmond's condition worsened rapidly. In addition to the painful phlegmons he developed dysentery.

At the same time he began behaving more and more like a child.

"You should trade your soup for bread," I advised

him, "and eat the bread only when it's a few days old."

He would say yes, but the minute I turned my back he gulped it all down.

By this time I had grown very weak myself and my legs were full of water — my whole body, in fact — so that it was difficult for me to stand up and help him.

+ + +

One day I was caught as I was sneaking into the toilet with Brachmond's blanket to wash it out in secret.

"Where's the filthy swine? Take him away! Out to room 4!"

As preparations were being made to transport my friend, I tottered back to his bunk to offer him some words of consolation. The whole time I felt as if I was about to break down any moment.

What awaited me there was the worst and most difficult experience of all my time in Dachau. My friend was out of his mind. He was babbling incoherently. Nevertheless he recognized me and suddenly began reproaching me with great bitterness. On what account I never understood, for suddenly everything went black. I said something and heard that I wasn't saying what I had intended to.

With effort I crept back to my bunk, slid under the blanket, was still able to register that Brachmond was being carried out past me, and then suddenly I found myself in a different world.

+ + +

I don't know what psychologists will think about what I am going to try to describe now:

All at once I had no contact with my surroundings. I had thoughts in my head, internal thoughts, but my thinking lacked concepts and seemed to me to have no influence on my external actions. I was incapable of coming up with even one verbal designation for something. In my mind I saw objects before me, and knew what they were, but I could not put a name to a single one.

While this was happening I thought about the state I was in as if from the outside, as if I weren't involved. At first the thought came to me that I had died and was in eternity. Then I suddenly thought I had lost my mind. Still huddled under the blanket, I tried to whisper a few words, and I heard that I was talking nonsense.

Now I knew: I've gone crazy. It's all over . . .

+ + +

I must have lain there for a good two hours. And sensed that very, very gradually the hideous state of being split in two was receding.

Suddenly there was a knock at the half-open window right next to my head. Then I heard the voice of Batty Esch: "Brachmond is dead . . . just now . . . in my arms . . ."

Now I started to cry and couldn't stop . . .

Then I felt I had my wits about me again. And prayed the *De Profundis* for my dead friend.

+ + +

When we report for bandaging the next day, the priests are turned away.

A new regulation from the camp authorities decrees: Priests are to receive no more medical treatment.

A few days later, however, the regulation is being interpreted to mean that attendants will put dressings on our sores, but otherwise not concern themselves with us.

For the moment that brought with it one advantage: Once again, and despite being a bag of water, I got my whole spoonful of soup . . .

Dead End

More and more, all of barrack 7 in the infirmary block took on the character that had previously limited to room 4: a dead end. The incurably sick from all the different wards ended up with us, along with all those "suffering from unclean, evil-smelling, or otherwise unpleasant ailments," and finally all priests were automatically sent to us, too. As a result the camp authorities could show spotlessly clean infirmary barracks to all visitors, and beds made up with white linen . . .

About that time 22 "advanced cases" were assigned to us from the overcrowded tuberculosis ward, and we were jammed in with them as well.

"Because of the danger of infection, speaking to the TB patients is prohibited," announced the man on room duty.

A young Pole on the room duty roster was not ill-disposed toward me. I had told him about his homeland, which I had already found appealing in many respects.

It was due to his efforts that I was finally moved down to the lowest tier of the bunks.

"At least you can die a more peaceful death here," he said. "And the fellow next to you is also a clergyman."

"Is there no treatment for water in the body?"

"There are mercury injections," he replied. "But not in this barrack. And I can't call the attendant, because priests aren't allowed to have treatment any more."

Noticing my disappointed expression, he ran his hand over my painfully swollen body and added consolingly, "It won't be today . . ."

+ + +

The next evening I couldn't move at all anymore. I had to lie on my back, and with every movement I felt how the water was impeding my heart. That night would be my last.

I had said farewell to Batty Esch through the window. He wasn't allowed in, since he was from room 4.

In Dachau one was at peace with God in any case. My Polish neighbor secretly gave me absolution for the last time. I can truly say that never in my life have I felt so close to heaven.

Then I thought once more of Luxembourg, of my dear family at home. And I recited to the Lord the long list of convictions for which I was willing to sacrifice my life for Him.

Renewed Hope

I must have lost consciousness then for several hours, for when I came to again it was the middle of the night.

Next to me I heard voices whispering.

"Give it to me!"

"You stupid idiot, that's the wrong injection!"

"Doesn't matter, there wasn't any other! And believe me I'm not risking it a second time . . ."

I lay absolutely still. Any movement at all could mean death.

Then someone pinched me in the thigh. I felt a stabbing pain.

+ + +

Not for long. Soon I was awakened by a dreadful need to urinate.

With all the caution I could muster I slid to the

ground and crawled on my hands and feet to the toilet, in terrible pain.

That night I got no more rest. I would estimate that I grew lighter by some 15 or 16 quarts . . . I knew already after the second trip that I was saved.

In the morning I wanted to thank my friend. "I don't know what you're talking about," was all he said. Was it out of caution, or do I owe my life to another?

I don't know to the present day.

"Have they taken Brachmond away yet?" That was my first question to Batty Esch when he said good morning to me through the window. I said nothing about what I had gone through during the night. In Dachau everyone kept his suffering to himself.

"The corpses aren't gone yet. But Brachmond is lying at the very bottom of the pile, and you can't see much of him at all."

I didn't even try to get up, since I already knew what a pile of naked corpses looked like. After their gold teeth had been knocked out, the dead of a given day were stacked like firewood in front of the barrack until the crematorium commando came with a cart to get them.

+ + +

"25487, come with me for interrogation!"

My heart skipped a beat. It might mean something good. At any rate it was a sign that someone was troubling himself about me.

"The man can't stand up," the fellow on duty explained.

"Then he can't be released either," snapped a Gestapo official who was standing in the doorway, the first civilian I had ever seen in the camp. "Where is the son of a bitch?"

"Here!" I called out as loud as I could. And all at once I was standing upright.

I threw my blanket around myself and struggled to follow the official into the washroom.

There I was allowed to sit on one of the toilets, and the interrogation began.

"What would you do if you were released?"

I thought my heart would burst. I made an enormous effort to gather my thoughts, poor as they were, since I sensed immediately what the man was getting at.

"I would ask my bishop to grant me a leave of absence for health reasons," I said cautiously.

"And then? — Then you'd put your bleeding cassock back on, wouldn't you, and the whole masquerade would start all over again! I've heard enough."

He left, and I tottered back to my bunk, feeling ambivalent about what had happened. How far could I have gone? And now all the best answers occurred to me. But it was too late, and I had no regrets.

All the same I felt enormously consoled by the awareness that in one place or another someone was working on my release.

+ + +

That thought gave me courage.

After a few days I was able to get up for an hour or

two. Then my favorite thing to do was go out in front of the barrack and sit in the sun with Batty Esch.

+ + +

We didn't see much of Wampach. Room 3 had a strict attendant who didn't allow his people to have any contact with the inmates of other rooms.

One day Wampach's name was called out. He had to fall into formation with the others and off they went to the invalid block.

Why to the invalid block? A new regulation decreed that prisoners who were classified as still unfit for work after a stay in the infirmary would not return to their regular barrack but be sent to the "invalid block," which was segregated from the rest of the camp. In this respect the priests once again received special treatment: on being released from the infirmary all of them, even if they were completely fit again, were moved to the invalid block.

In itself that wouldn't have mattered so much. But transports of prisoners left the invalid block at regular intervals, prisoners who — by what route nobody could say — ended up at the crematorium . . .

So then we knew: Reckoning from the date you were assigned to the invalid block, you had little chance of remaining alive for more than a few weeks.

+ + +

A few days later it was Batty Esch's turn, and I was left alone in the infirmary.

I now spent more time with my friend Maurice de

Backer, a priest from Brussels whose deeply pious and wholly unaffected nature did me good.

During that time a prisoner who brought the food passed on news about several other Luxembourgers in the camp: Franz Clément was dead; Monsignor Origer was still in the invalid block. Pastor Dupong had been assigned not to the priests' barrack but to barrack 14, and had been given a work assignment. Thorn and Noppeney had been sick, but were now better.

+ + +

On July 23 the time came for de Backer and me to be released from the infirmary.

I had recovered enough to be able to walk a bit — with the shuffling gait and sluggish movements typical of our condition.

As we stood in formation waiting to march away, Emil Schaus called out to me. So he was back from the external ski commando at Liebhof and had landed in the infirmary, too.

"Edema," I thought to myself when I saw his puffy and swollen face.

"Where are Batty and the others?"

"Already in the invalid block. I'm the last one left."

A quick handshake was all there was time for; then we marched off.

+ + +

The original invalid barrack had now grown into three: 23, 25, and 27. Like the infirmary block, they were separated from the rest of the camp by a barbed-wire fence.

It was a great consolation for us to re-encounter the other survivors here. We consisted of Monsignor Origer, Batty, Esch, Wampach and I, since Father Stoffels, Becker, and Brachmond were already in eternity.

I joined Monsignor Origer in Room 1. Esch and Wampach were assigned to beds in Room 3.

The "robing ceremony" was extremely simple. We were given a shirt, and that was it. Each of us had to sew ours together so that it was more or less in one piece. Prudish people stitched the sides together or lengthened theirs by sewing on bits of old rags, which they got from the prisoner on room duty in exchange for bread. But only the newcomers bothered.

+ + +

In barrack 27 there are no straw sacks. We sleep on the slats of the bunks.

Everyone gets one blanket and has the choice to use it either as a cover or a mattress.

As a "new arrival" I have to climb up to the third tier. It's horribly difficult for me. First I have to take one knee and lift it with my hands onto the foot end of the bottom bunk; then I hold on to the foot of the middle bed and, using all my strength, pull myself up. Now I have both knees on the foot end of the bottom bunk. At this point I have to stop and rest. Next I lift one foot up to the same level — using my hands again, since my legs are so heavy with water that they won't move on their own — and pull myself up with my arms until I'm standing on the edge of the bottom bunk. Then the whole operation has to be repeated on the middle tier, until I finally fall onto the top slats trembling from the exertion, with my heart pounding. It is a catastrophe to discover that one of the slats is missing, stolen by one of my dear neighbors, since the slats simply lie unattached across the iron rods below, and there are not enough of them to go around. It is not such an easy matter in that case to position the few remaining slats, which keep shifting around, so that you can lie down without being in constant danger of falling through to the bunk below.

+ + +

In the invalid barrack we aren't much affected by the camp routine. We get up at 4 a.m., and our coffee is delivered at about half past, after which we are ordered out of the barrack until the midday meal. We have our own private "head count" on the barrack street. There we sit, lie, or stand around no matter whether it is raining or the sun is shining. In order to sit you take your wooden clogs off, put them next to one another on the ground and sit on them, with your arms around your knees. It is strictly forbidden to lean your back against the barrack wall.

The afternoon proceeds in exactly the same manner, as everyone tries to find a place and a position where his sores and boils won't be pressed against the hard gravel.

+ + +

I re-encounter a dear friend in the invalid barrack, Father de Coninck, a Jesuit from Brussels whom I got to know through the Catholic Film Bureau. He is a relatively recent arrival and still in possession of his full strength.

Along with Maurice de Backer, Father de Coninck joins our little group and becomes our spiritual and mental support in this final, desolate stage of debilitation.

From now on we gather every morning after breakfast at a quiet end of the barrack street and pray together as inconspicuously as we can. If someone approaches too closely, we start speaking of trivial matters.

Then Father de Coninck proposes some points for consideration, which we try to discuss informally. As we talk we sit on our clogs in pairs, leaning up against one another's backs.

After that "Mass" begins. Each of us knows some of it by heart. The one we like to pray best is the Luxembourg Mass of the Virgin, "*Ave spes nostra.*"

+ + +

One morning Father de Coninck pulls out a cellophane bag labeled "vitamin C" from a fold in his shirt. In the good old days it was possible to buy such vitamin pills at the camp store.

Through the cellophane the shimmer of a piece of consecrated Host was visible, barely half an inch long. We all had difficulty hiding our excitement.

"Don't give us away," said de Coninck. "A German priest from barrack 26 has sent the Lord to us."

We decide to keep this most precious treasure among us for the time being and then to divide it among ourselves for the day when each of us is put on a transport.

Those were days of celebration. Now when we spoke the prayers of the Mass together, Father de Coninck held the Host inconspicuously in his hand. How much consolation that brought to the hearts of the tormented priests, how much courage and readiness to sacrifice, cannot be expressed in words.

+ + +

Day and night we were confronted with the specter of "transport."

Every Saturday between 50 and 100 men were taken away. Some of them reacted with extreme distress, while others displayed no feelings at all and just did what they were told. A few even emitted a demented cackle when the command was given to start marching.

Try as we might, we could never work out any pattern for how the inmates of the invalid block were chosen for transport. Everything suggested that the names were taken randomly from the card file.

+ + +

It is Saturday, August 1, 1942.

A prisoner carrying food summons me mysteriously to the barbed-wire fence of our block. Two prisoners are standing there talking. I loiter near them as if by chance. They introduce themselves as university students, members of the Catholic Action group in Vienna. "Schmitz said to tell you that your name is on the list for transport next Saturday. He doesn't know about the others . . . Someone is prepared to switch your names from the list of the living to the dead in the card file. Then you'll never be called up for transport. The price is one and a half loaves of bread."

"You'll get our answer tomorrow," I say and rush off to my friends. They were in total disagreement.

"The price is too high," said Wampach. "I can't possibly save a loaf and a half of bread! And finally we have no guarantee at all that our names will actually be taken off the list for transport. If I have to die, then I really don't care whether it's from starvation or gas . . ."

For my part I couldn't possibly hesitate, since my name was already on the list for the coming Saturday. Batty Esch was willing to join in, too.

"Since you're already on the list," he said, "we'll buy you off first. I'll help you fast; we'll share our bread, and next week you'll help me."

"I'll help you both out," said Monsignor Origer. "I demand nothing more from life. My work is done."

When I recall today the sacrifice these noble men were willing to make, I have to fight back tears. Back then we weren't so emotional. We simply shook his hand without a word.

+ + +

The next day Esch and I passed across half a loaf of bread with our answer, as a down payment. We had cut it into small pieces that would fit through the barbed-wire fence.

"On Tuesday night the first one of you will disappear from the card file of the living," we were told.

I wasn't so terribly optimistic about the whole business: If the boy was caught falsifying the records, then it was all over for both him and us.

Nevertheless I couldn't risk any hesitation, since I faced certain death in the clutches of the transport commando in only a few days.

Only one thought crossed my mind fleetingly: If I did happen to be released then they would search for my name in vain, and find it only in the card file of the dead. Instead of being reported as released, I would be listed as dead . . .

But at such a point who would still indulge in that kind of hope?

+ + +

During the night from Tuesday to Wednesday I couldn't sleep a wink.

Officially I was in the process of "dying" . . .

I was far from certain whether this official death might not have entirely unforeseen consequences.

And would the maneuver be successful?

I tried to pray, trembling from excitement, physical weakness, and exhaustion.

Released

Wednesday, August 5, 1942.

We fall in for the head count.

The man standing in front of me is Baron X from Paris. He has diarrhea, and the watery feces are running down his legs. A neighbor utters a curse about the stench and punches him in the midsection.

I just have time to say, "Wait and see, it will be your turn some day," when the SS man arrives to count us.

As I catch sight of him the thought flashes through my head: If I were going to be released, this would be the last possible day . . .

I am about to laugh at myself for such a childish hope when I hear someone call out my number: 25487!

That can mean only one thing: release!

+ + +

For a moment I didn't budge. I couldn't grasp what

was happening and was incapable of moving.

The SS man and barrack head prisoner immediately start swearing loudly at me. A fellow prisoner expresses his envy the only way he can think of, by giving me a kick as a farewell gift. It brings me back to reality.

I stumble through the ranks to the front of our group, looking around for my friends. They are standing too far away for me to catch sight of them, though. I can hardly grasp that I have to leave them like this.

+ + +

I'm given a pair of trousers, which I have to hold up with both hands, since it isn't allowed to go all the way forward with just a shirt on. Then we head out to the camp street.

Somehow I'm unable to follow the SS man, however. After only a few steps dizziness overcomes me and I simply fall down.

"Pick up your bones and wait here. I have to get someone from barrack 25, too!"

The other fortunate soul was an old man, a cripple, who, I learned later, had been sent to the camp only a few days earlier by mistake.

My guardian angel gave me an inspiration: I leaned on the old man and pretended to be helping him . . .

+ + +

One reason was because I was well aware that sick and severely debilitated prisoners were simply not released. So it was crucial that I summon every last ounce of energy to conceal how weak I was.

The closer we got to the infirmary, the lower my hopes sank. In the state I was in I would never pass the doctor's inspection!

+ + +

The SS doctor is not there. The man in charge of us bellows for the prisoner acting temporarily as his deputy.

When the attendant appears he immediately objects, "I'm not permitted to issue a release certificate."

"Listen here, you son of a bitch! This is my day off. Do you think I'm going to stand around with these two guys all afternoon? You fill out those forms right now and stamp them, understand? Whatever lies you have to tell the doctor is your problem!"

A brutal punch to the man's head gave the order the required emphasis.

White with fear, the unfortunate prisoner opened the record book.

I undressed and stepped on the scale. The grand total came to just over 100 pounds.

The SS man wouldn't even let the attendant take a look, however, but dictated what he was supposed to write down: "One hundred fifty pounds, understood? And top fit! No open sores, no lice, no scabies. Well nourished, and in great shape overall!" Within seconds we are outside again. Only now do I start to believe that I will actually be released.

+ + +

The usual ceremonies follow.

My clothes hang in folds on me. The personal items I had to turn in 18 months earlier are returned, with not a single thing missing. I get back the money I had on me, accurate down to the last penny.

In the political office they spout the party line at us, with the usual warnings.

"As for you," the official tells me, "you are being released from the camp only on probation; you will remain in protective custody and must report every second day to the security police in Luxembourg until the end of the war!"

Everything was all right by me . . .

+ + +

Then we are standing outside, in front of the main gate.

A small van took us to the railway station, with a guard still accompanying us. Across the street from the station is the post office. I asked the SS man for permission to send a telegram home and lurched across the street. I could feel the man was observing me.

Now I was standing at the bottom of three steps leading up to the entrance. I hadn't considered that. I wouldn't make it up them . . . The guard would become suspicious . . . and might take me back to camp with him.

To gain some time, I pretended to be interested in the contents of a glass display case next to the entrance, which contained all kinds of notices, and watched the guard behind me in the reflection. For a moment he looked away, and in that instant I crawled up the steps on all fours.

+ + +

I managed to get into the train without difficulty. One person pulled me up by my arms, while someone else pushed from behind. Although the train was over-crowded, a woman conductor immediately found me a seat. Should I attribute this to my clerical garb or my shaved head? Probably it was both together.

Not until the train starts moving do I feel that I am free. And can hardly comprehend that I can now do whatever I want . . .

+ + +

The next morning I stood at the altar again for the first time. But it was also the last time for a good while, since my health now suffered a total collapse.

That was on the 6th of August, the anniversary of the day I first celebrated Mass.

Biographical Note

Jean Bernard was born in 1907 as the sixth of ten children in a well-known family of merchants in Luxembourg. He studied philosophy and theology first at the University of Louvain in Belgium, then at the Catholic seminary in Luxembourg. After his ordination as a priest in 1933 he completed his Ph.D. at Louvain.

In 1929 Bernard became involved in the work of the Church on films and the cinema, and in 1934 he became general secretary of the International Catholic Cinema Office, which had its headquarters in Brussels. He remained in this position until the German invasion of Belgium and Luxembourg. In June 1940 the German Gestapo closed the office and seized its files. The premises became the headquarters of the German military police; later the site, once a private chapel, was used by the SS as a torture chamber.

After the collapse of France, Bernard worked under the aegis of the still functioning Luxembourg authorities — and with the agreement of the German occupiers — to organize the return of the many Luxembourg citizens who had fled to western France before the advancing German army. This effort involved supervising convoys of buses and trucks and required Bernard to make eleven trips between Paris and Luxembourg, sometimes in dangerous proximity to battle zones around the forts of the Maginot Line. After the operation was completed, Bernard was arrested by the Germans on January 6, 1941.

The author himself was uncertain of the real reasons behind his arrest. In the questions put to him during interrogation he was accused of having "incited" the returning Luxembourg citizens with "separatist propaganda" on various occasions, and to have carried letters and messages on his trips between Luxembourg and France. Although this may have been the pretext for Bernard's arrest, the underlying reason is likely to have been simply that the newly installed German civilian occupation and the Gestapo saw another opportunity to remove some well-known figures from public life and thereby to break Luxembourgers' will to resist. This best explains why Bernard was sent to a concentration camp. Priests were specially targeted because the leaders of the occupation regarded the Luxembourg clergy — with some justification — as one of the centers of patriotic resistance for the population, the vast majority of which was devoutly Catholic. While there is no direct evidence that Bernard's work for the

Cinema Office also played a role — the Nazis referred to it as "the Vatican's headquarters in the fight against German films" — it is probably safe to assume that it did.

If the investigation and Bernard's interrogation had produced evidence of his guilt, i.e. evidence that he had violated existing laws or ordinances, then his case would no doubt have been handled by the courts, and he would have received a prison sentence. It would have been limited to a certain number of years, however. Lacking such proof, the German authorities fell back on the familiar tactic of forcing the accused into a situation where the only way he could avoid incriminating himself would have been to betray his homeland and his own convictions, a "conversion" that the occupiers could have exploited to great effect. Once Bernard had declared his loyalty to church and country, the Gestapo could regard him as an opponent of Luxembourg's annexation and thus as a potential enemy in wartime who had to be "taken out of circulation." That was how "protective custody" and "reeducation" in the notorious concentration camps were defined in legal terms.

Very little is known even today about the background of Bernard's highly unusual "leave" in February 1942 and his no less extraordinary release. Certain is only that both friends and family members had made efforts on his behalf, and that his release from Dachau occurred without the knowledge of the Gestapo in Luxembourg. The most effective intervention probably came from his oldest brother, who was then living in Paris, at a time when the German ambassador Otto von Abetz was striving to create an atmosphere of cooperation. Bernard always gave great credit to the high-ranking German army officers there for never demanding political favors or concessions from his brother in return for obtaining his release.

After leaving Dachau "on probation," Bernard spent a year in a sanatorium in a state of extreme debility and exhaustion. Constantly bothered by the Gestapo in Luxembourg, who clearly resented being bypassed on the matter of his release, Father Bernard then moved to a monastery in a rural area, where he experienced the liberation by Allied forces in October 1944.

Appointed editor of the Catholic daily newspaper *Luxemburger Wort,* Bernard also immediately took up his work on films again. He was elected president of the International Catholic Cinema Office in 1947, a position that he still held in 1962 when his memoir was first published in book form. When symptoms of an illness he had contracted in Dachau recurred, he had to step down as editor of the newspaper but remained on its editorial staff. Elected to the clerical board of the Catholic Apostolate of the Laity in his country and made an honorary canon of the Luxembourg Cathedral in 1955, Bernard was named a papal privy chamberlain in 1958. He served as a consultant to the Papal Commission for Film, Radio and Television and as a member of the Preparatory Secretariat for the Press and the Entertainment World in advance of the Second Vatican Council. Monsignor Bernard further chaired the Commission for the Persecuted Church within the Conference of International Catholic

Organizations. He was made a Chevalier de l'Ordre de la Couronne de Chêne (Luxembourg), a Chevalier de l'Ordre de Léopold (Belgium) and awarded the Stella della Solidarietà (Italy).

He died at the age of 87 on September 1, 1994.

Jean Bernard, circa 1930s

With Pope John Paul II, 1979

ROBERT ROYAL is president of the Faith & Reason Institute in Washington, D.C. His books include: *The God that Did Not Fail: How Religion Built and Sustains the West* (2006), *The Catholic Martyrs of the Twentieth Century: A Comprehensive Global History* (2000), and *1492 And All That: Political Manipulations of History* (1992). His articles have appeared in numerous scholarly journals and other publications, including *First Things, Communio, The Wilson Quarterly, The Washington Post,* and *The Wall Street Journal.*

DEBORAH LUCAS SCHNEIDER has translated several works of 20th-century German history, including *The Wehrmacht: History, Myth, Reality* (2006), *From Athens to Auschwitz: The Uses of History* (2005), and *Germany: A New History* (2001).

MORE FINE CATHOLIC BOOKS FROM

ZACCHEUS PRESS

A Key to the Doctrine of the Eucharist by **Abbot Vonier.**
196 pages, $14.95. "One of the few classics in
Catholic theology composed in English. This book
should never be out of print." —Avery Cardinal Dulles

Our Lady and the Church by **Hugo Rahner, S.J. 152
pages, $12.95.** "This marvelous work is one of the
most important theological rediscoveries of the 20th
century." —Joseph Ratzinger (Pope Benedict XVI)

Christ, the Life of the Soul by **Blessed Columba Marmion;
Introduction by Father Benedict Groeschel. 532 pages,
pbk: $24.95; hardcover: $49.95.** "Read this: it is the
pure doctrine of the Church." —Pope Benedict XV

*Union with God: Letters of Spiritual Direction by Blessed
Columba Marmion.* **233 pages, $14.95.** "May a wide-
spread rediscovery of the spiritual writings of
Blessed Columba Marmion help priests and laity to
grow in union with Christ." —Pope John Paul II

Hammer & Fire: Way to Contemplative Happiness by
Fr. Raphael Simon. 323 pages, $15.95. "Clear, simple,
and beautiful wisdom." —Fr. Matthew Lamb, Ave
Maria University

**To order, visit www.ZaccheusPress.com
or call 1-970-416-6672 (9am to 5pm MST)**